THE **TESTING** SERIES

ARMY BARB **TEST QUESTIONS**

Orders: Please contact How2become Ltd, Suite 2, 50 Churchill Square Business Centre, Kings Hill, Kent ME19 4YU.

You can order via the e-mail address info@how2become.co.uk or through Gardners Books at Gardners.com.

ISBN: 9781907558498

First published 2011

Typeset for How2become Ltd by Molly Hill, Canada.

Printed in Great Britain for How2become Ltd
by Bell & Bain Ltd, 303 Burnfield Road, Thornliebank, Glasgow G46 7UQ.

CONTENTS

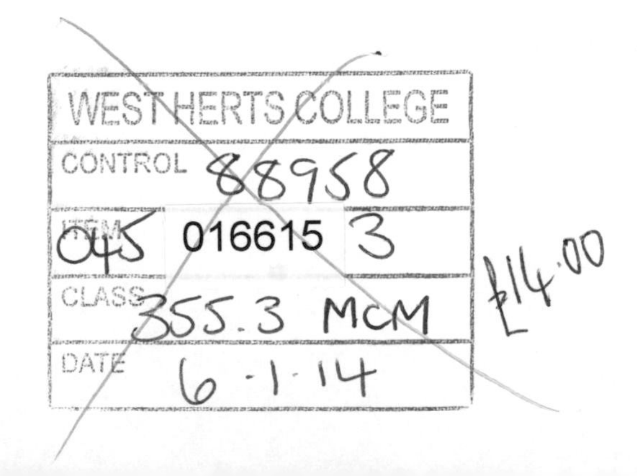

INTRODUCTION

Dear Sir/Madam,

Welcome to your new guide: Army BARB Test Questions. This guide contains lots of sample test questions that are appropriate for anyone who is applying to join the British Army.

The selection test for the Army is designed to assess potential employees 'suitability' for specific posts. The higher scores you achieve, the more job opportunities you will have at your disposal. Whilst the minimum pass mark for entry in the Army is 26, a candidate will need to score far higher if he or she wishes to join a regiment such as the Royal Electrical and Mechanical Engineers. The key to success is to try your hardest to get 100% correct answers in the test that you are undertaking. If you aim for 100% in your preparation, then you are far more likely to achieve the trade or career that you want. We have deliberately supplied you with lots of sample questions to assist you. It is crucial that when you get a question wrong, you take the time to find out why you got it wrong. Understanding the question is very important.

You will find that the more practice you undertake in the build up to the real test, the better you will perform on the day.

Good luck and best wishes,

The how2become team

The How2become team

PREFACE
BY RICHARD MCMUNN

It's probably important that I start off by explaining a little bit about myself, my background, and also why I'm suitably qualified to help you pass the selection tests that form part of the British Army.

At the time of writing I am 39 years old and live in the sea-side town of Whitstable which is located on the North Kent coast. I left school at the usual age of 16 and joined the Royal Navy, serving on-board HMS Invincible as part of 800 Naval Air Squadron which formed part of the Fleet Air Arm. There I was, at the age of 16, travelling the world and working as an engineer on Sea Harrier jets! It was fantastic and I loved every minute of it. After four years I left the Royal Navy and joined Kent Fire and Rescue Service as a firefighter. Over the next 17 years I worked my way up through the ranks to the position of Assistant Divisional Officer. During my time in the Fire Service I spent a lot of time working as an instructor at the Fire Brigade Training Centre. I was also involved in the selection process for assessing candidates who wanted to join the job as a firefighter. Therefore, my knowledge and experience gained so far in life has been invaluable in helping people like you to pass any type of selection process. I am sure you will find this guide an invaluable resource during your preparation for the Army BARB Test.

I have always been fortunate in the fact that I persevere at everything I do. I understand that if I keep working hard in life then I will always be successful; or I will achieve whatever it is that I want to achieve. This is an important lesson that I want you to take on-board straight away. If you work hard and persevere, then success will come your way. The same rule applies whilst applying for a career in the Armed Forces; if you work hard and try lots of test questions, then you will be successful.

Finally, it is very important that you believe in your own abilities. It does not matter if you have no qualifications. It does not matter if are currently weak in the area of psychometric testing. What does matter is self-belief, self-discipline and a genuine desire to improve and become successful.

Best wishes,

Richard McMunn

Richard McMunn

CHAPTER 1
THE REASONING TEST

Within this guide I have provided you with a number of sample test questions to help you prepare for the real test. Please note that these are not the exact questions that you will be required to sit on the day. However, they are provided as a useful practice tool in order to help focus your mind on the type of tests you will be sitting. It is also important to point out that during the real test you will be required to answer the questions on a computer screen and how they will be presented will be different to how they are formatted within this guide.

Take a look at the explanations provided and make sure you fully understand what is involved before attempting the practice questions. Once you have completed the practice questions it is important that you take note of where you have gone wrong. Learn from any mistakes as this will help you to further improve your scores during the real test.

Reasoning tests form an integral part of the BARB selection tests within the British Army selection process. These tests are relatively simple to understand once you fully appreciate what is required. The reasoning tests are basically a form of problem solving and you will be asked a number of questions, usually about a relationship between two people. For example, you could be asked a question along the following lines:

Sample question

Richard is taller than Steven. Who is shorter?

The answer in this case would be Steven as the statement suggests that Richard is taller than Steven. Therefore Steven is the shorter of the two.

Answer: Steven

Here is another example:

Sample question

Mark is not as wealthy as Jane. Who has less money?

Answer: Mark.

The statement suggests that Mark is not as wealthy as Jane therefore suggesting that Jane has more money. Mark therefore has less money and is not as wealthy as Jane.

When you are answering these questions it is important that you READ each question thoroughly. The questions are relatively simple to answer but they can catch you out if you do not understand exactly what the question is asking.

TIPS FOR PASSING THE REASONING TESTS

When you attend the careers office to sit the BARB test you may be asked to take the test on a computer. The computer version of the test will require you to use 'touch screen' answers, which means that instead of using a pen and paper to mark down your answers you will have to touch the computer screen instead. Whilst this is far quicker than writing down your answers, you will need to understand the questions fully before giving your answer.

The question on the screen may appear as follows:

Steven runs faster than Jane

Once you have read the statement you will then need to touch the screen to obtain the question. Make certain that you remember the statement as when you touch the screen it will disappear and you will be given two choices of answer as follows:

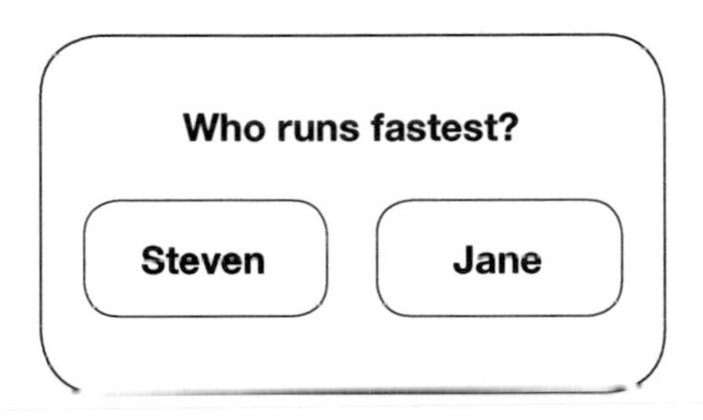

Once the question appears you will then be required to touch the screen in order to indicate your answer. Can you remember what the question was? My tip is to repeat the statement at least three times in your head before touching the screen to obtain the question. Once the question appears you can repeat the statement to yourself that ***Steven runs faster than Jane*** and therefore provide yourself with the answer to the question – ***Steven is the fastest.***

Once you fully understand what is required, move on to exercise 1 on the following page. You have 5 minutes in which to answer the 15 questions. Please note that the time limit placed on this exercise will not be the same as the one set during the real BARB test.

Once you have completed the exercise make sure you check thoroughly any questions you got wrong. It is important to do this so that you can improve your scores during the real test

BARB TEST PRACTICE QUESTIONS

REASONING TEST - EXERCISE 1

1. Marcus is not as bright as Andrew.

Who is brighter?

Answer

2. Sharon is taller than Sheila

Who is the tallest?

Answer

3. Pauline is stronger than Beverley.

Who is the weaker of the two?

Answer

4. Gary is lighter than Frederick.

Who is the heavier?

Answer

5. The black car is faster than the white car.

Which car is the quickest?

Answer

6. Rachel runs faster than her sister Georgia.

Who runs the slowest?

Answer

7. David has more money than Arnold.

Who is the poorer?

Answer

8. Jill is weaker than Bill.

Who is the strongest?

Answer

9. Hayley sleeps for 10 hours and Julie sleeps for 650 minutes.

Who sleeps the longest?

Answer

10. Sadie's shoe size is 7 and Mary's is 9.

Who needs the larger size shoes?

Answer

11. George is sadder than Mark.

Who is the happier of the two?

Answer

12. Pete is faster than Rick.

Who is the slowest?

Answer

13. Jim is older than Brian.

Who is the youngest?

Answer

14. Katie eats slower than Lucy.

Who is the faster eater?

Answer

15. John finishes the race before Tony.

Who ran the slowest?

Answer

ANSWERS TO REASONING TEST - EXERCISE 1

1. Andrew
2. Sharon
3. Beverley
4. Frederick
5. The black car
6. Georgia
7. Arnold
8. Bill
9. Julie
10. Mary
11. Mark
12. Rick
13. Brian
14. Lucy
15. Tony

Now move on to Reasoning Test Exercise 2. You have 5 minutes to complete the 15 questions.

REASONING TEST - EXERCISE 2

1. The red car is twice as fast as the grey car.

Which car is slowest?

Answer

2. Julia is half the weight of her neighbour Jonathan.

Who is the heaviest?

Answer

3. Barry has been playing darts for three times longer than his team mate Paul.

Who has played for the least amount of time?

Answer

4. Jim passed his driving test in 1998 and his wife Gloria passed hers in 1989.

Who has held their driving licence the longest?

Answer

5. Darren lives 13 miles away from his place of work. Jessica's workplace is 12 miles away from her home?

Who lives the furthest away from their place of work?

Answer

6. Rupert has a motorbike which cost £6,450 and Mark has a motorbike which cost £5,654.

Who has the least expensive motorbike?

Answer

7. Ronald weighs slightly more than Peter.

Who is the lightest?

Answer

8. Stuart's house was built in August 1965 and his girlfriend Margaret's house was built in January 1965.

Whose house is the oldest?

Answer

9. If Jen has £3.95 and Marcus has 295 pence, who has the least money?

Answer

10. Carol attends the doctor's surgery at 9am and leaves at 9.35am. Harriet attends the doctor's surgery at 9.35am and leaves at 10.09am.

Who stayed at the doctors for the least amount of time?

Answer

11. Ben joined the Army on October the 3rd 1997 and left nine years later. Hannah joined the Army on January the 25th 1993 and left on January the 25th 2003.

Who stayed in the Army the longest?

Answer

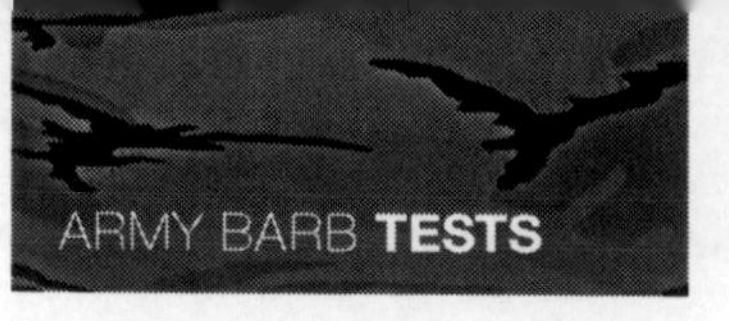

12. In 2005 a total of 11,400 people joined the Army. In the previous year a total 10,340 joined the Army.

In which of the two years did the Army recruit the least amount of people?

Answer

13. Abdi is wealthier than Maggie.

Who is the poorest?

Answer

14. Stuart rides his bike twice the speed of Simon.

Who rides their bike the fastest?

Answer

15. Michelle takes out a mortgage for £189,500 and Anthony takes out a mortgage for £198,200.

Who has the least amount to pay back?

Answer

Once again, take the time to check over your answers carefully correcting any that you have got wrong before moving onto the next exercise.

ANSWERS TO REASONING TEST - EXERCISE 2

1. The grey car
2. Jonathan
3. Paul
4. Gloria
5. Darren
6. Mark
7. Peter
8. Margaret's house
9. Marcus
10. Carol
11. Hannah
12. 2004
13. Maggie
14. Stuart
15. Michelle

Now move on to Reasoning Test Exercise 3. You have 5 minutes to complete the 15 questions.

REASONING TEST - EXERCISE 3

1. Bill gets 70%of his answers correct during the test whilst Sam got 25% incorrect.

Who achieved the highest score in the test?

Answer

2. Richard is not as happy as Graham.

Who is the happier?

Answer

3. William has a car that is half as fast as Bill.

Who has the slowest car?

Answer

4. Anthony can run twice as fast as Hillary.

Who is the slowest runner?

Answer

5. Jean was born in 1971 and Frank was born 3 years later.

Who is the eldest?

Answer

6. Peter washed his car for 90 minutes whereas Abdul washed his for 1 hour and twenty minutes.

Who washed his car for the longest?

Answer

7. Ahmed is more intelligent than Sinita.

Who is the brightest?

Answer

8. Mika passed his motorbike test 18 months ago whereas June passed her motorbike test 350 days ago.

Who passed their test first?

Answer

9. Fin carries five bags of shopping home and Dalton carries home seven.

Who has the least number of bags to carry?

Answer

10. Naomi arrives at work at 0834 hours and leaves at 1612 hours. Stuart arrives at work at 0915 hours and leaves at 1700 hours.

Who stayed at work for the least amount of time?

Answer

11. Preston weighs heavier than Paris.

Who is the lightest?

Answer

12. David is not as good as Brian.

Who is better?

Answer

13. Ricky is not as fast as Carlos.

Who is fastest?

Answer

14. Yasmin is sadder than Beatrice.

Who is happier?

Answer

15. Laurence is poorer than Gene.

Who is richer?

Answer

Once again, take the time to check over your answers carefully correcting any that you have got wrong before moving onto the next section of the BARB test.

ANSWERS TO REASONING TEST - EXERCISE 3

1. Sam
2. Graham
3. William
4. Hillary
5. Jean
6. Peter
7. Ahmed
8. Mika
9. Fin
10. Naomi
11. Paris
12. Brian
13. Carlos
14. Beatrice
15. Gene

CHAPTER 2
THE LETTER CHECKING TEST

When you come to sit the BARB test you will be asked to answer questions where you are required to check letters. The aim of this test is to see how fast you can check information that is presented before you. Whilst working in the Army you will be often required to carry out specific tasks which involve the accurate checking of information, equipment and data.

The following is an example of a letter checking question:

Sample question

P	I	O	T	S
p	N	K	t	u

How many letters match?

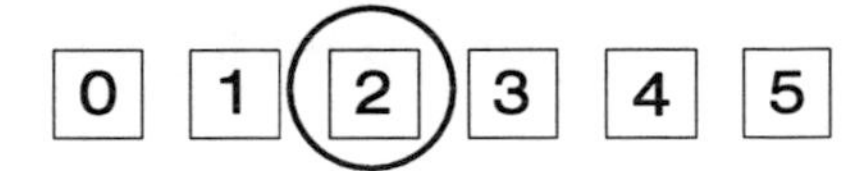

You can see from the above example that there are columns of letters. In the 1st and 4th box are letters that are identical, albeit one letter is a capital and the other is not. The other boxes contain different letters and therefore do not match. It is your task to identify how many pairs of letters match. In this case I have circled the correct answer for you as being 2 matching pairs.

During the real BARB test you will most probably be asked to sit the computer 'touch-screen' version of the test as opposed to writing down your answers.

When you carry out the test on the computer the question on the screen will be presented to you in a similar format to the following:

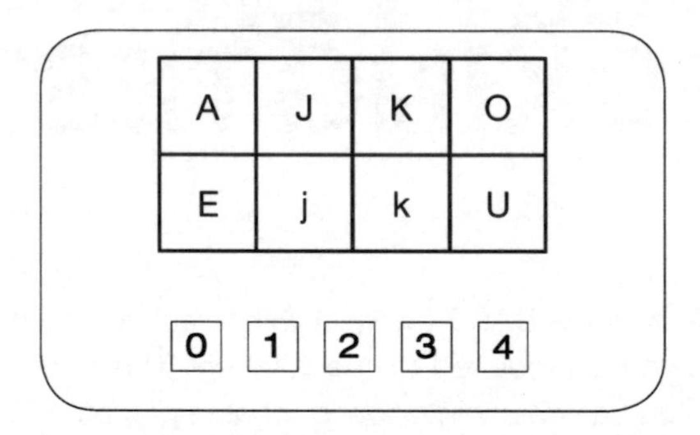

Below the provided letters will be a number of boxes giving you a choice of how many letters match. In this case the answer is 2 as the middle two columns of letters match, whereas the outer two do not. In this case you would touch the number '2' box as your answer. It is important that you work as quickly as possible as the more you score correct, the higher your result will be at the end. As always, deliberate and repetitive practice will serve well to increase your scores.

TIPS FOR IMPROVING YOUR SCORE ON THE LETTER CHECKING TEST

When answering these questions you may find it useful to scan each line downwards in turn and keep a check of how many are correct. When you have scanned the final 4th line you will know how many are correct and then you can touch the number on the screen that corresponds to the right answer.

You will have very little time to answer as many as you can during the real test so you need to work quickly but as accurately as possible. Look out for letters that are similar but not the same, such as:

Q and ***O***

G and ***Q***

P and ***q***

These are the ones that may catch you out so make sure you check carefully.

Now take a look at the first Letter Checking exercise on the following page and see how you get on. There are 15 questions and you have 5 minutes in which to answer them. Simply circle the correct answer with a pen or pencil.

LETTER CHECKING TEST - EXERCISE 1

Question 1

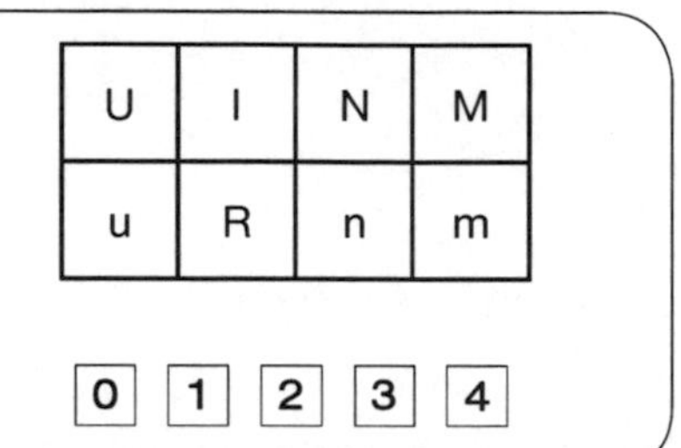

Question 2

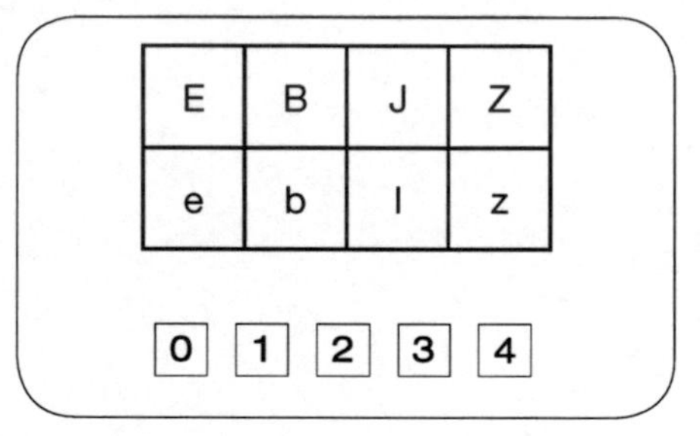

Question 3

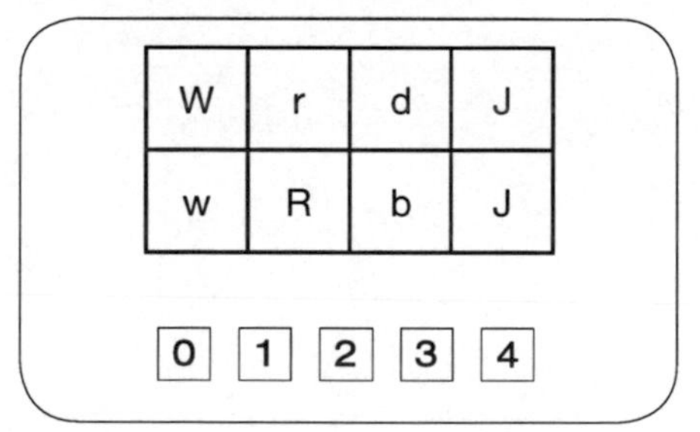

Question 4

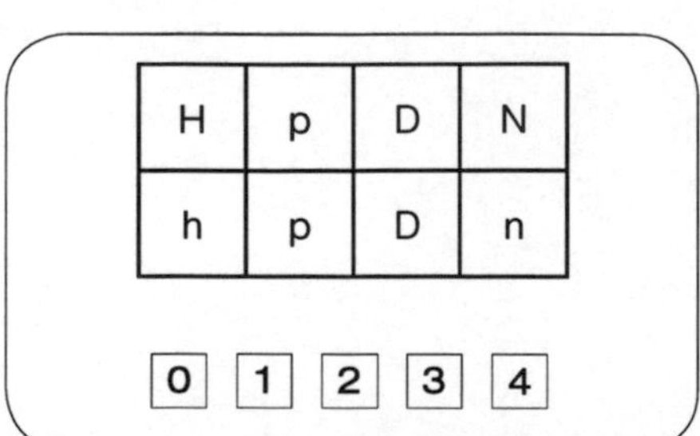

Question 5

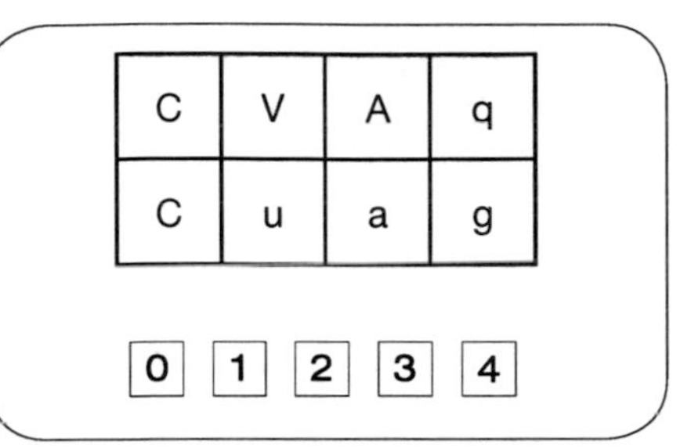

Question 6

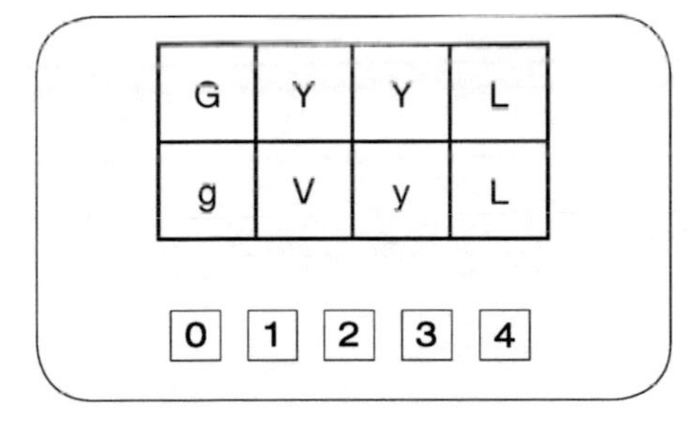

Question 7

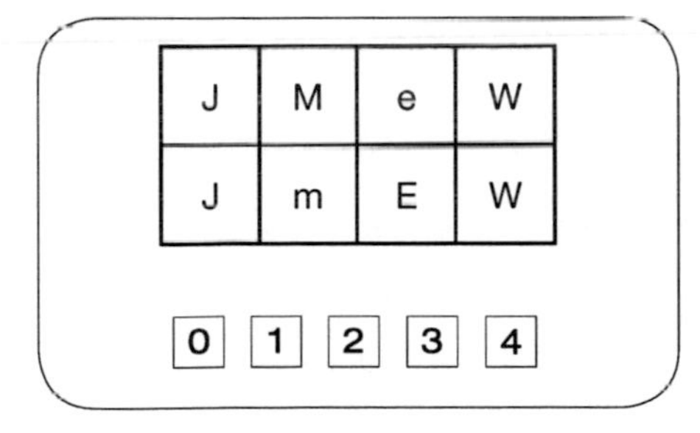

Question 8

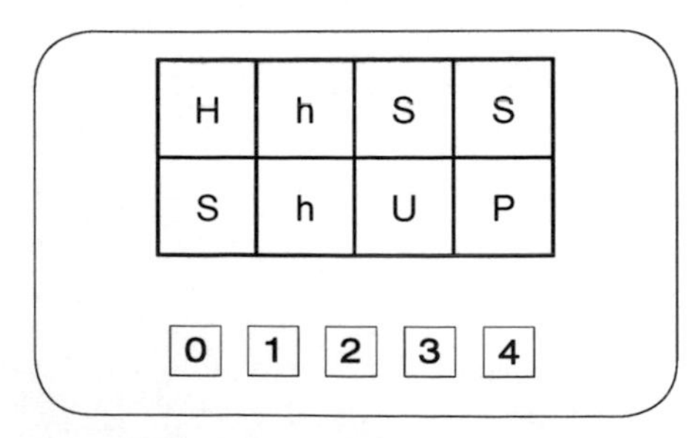

Question 9

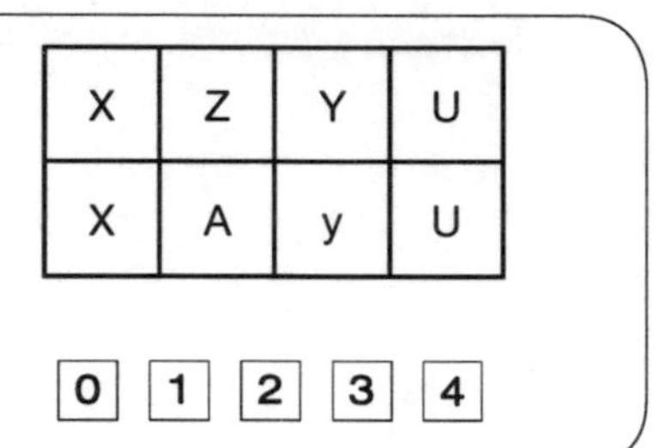

Question 10

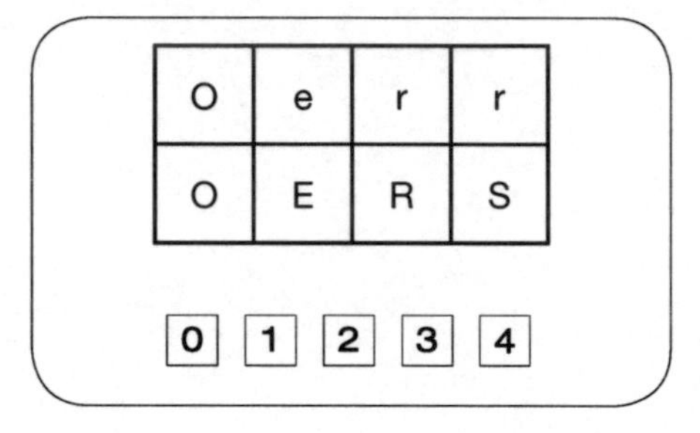

Question 11

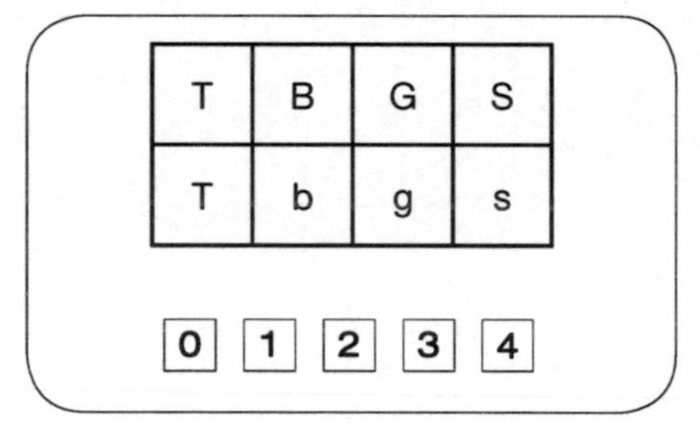

Question 12

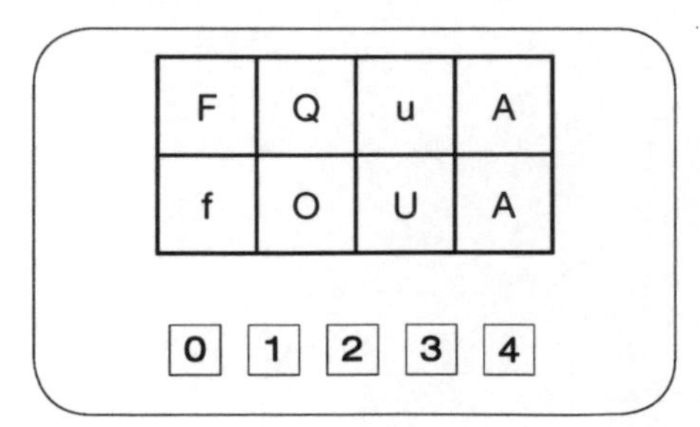

Question 13

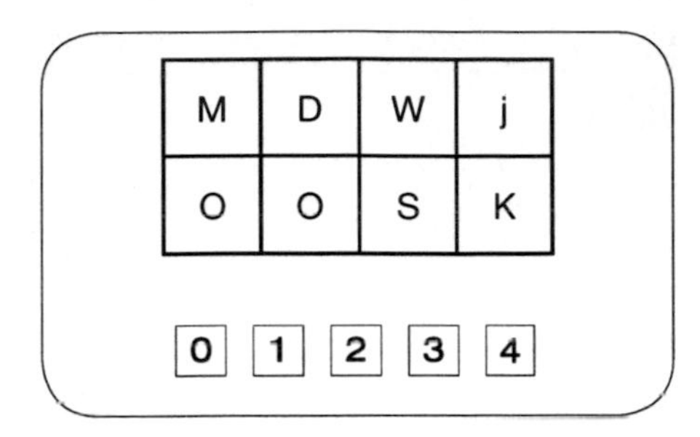

Question 14

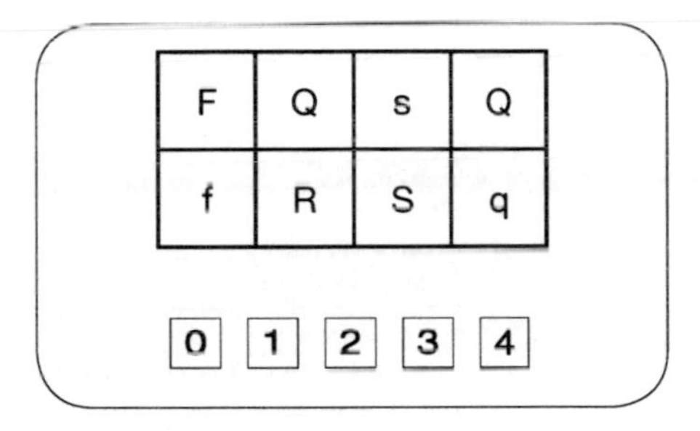

Question 15

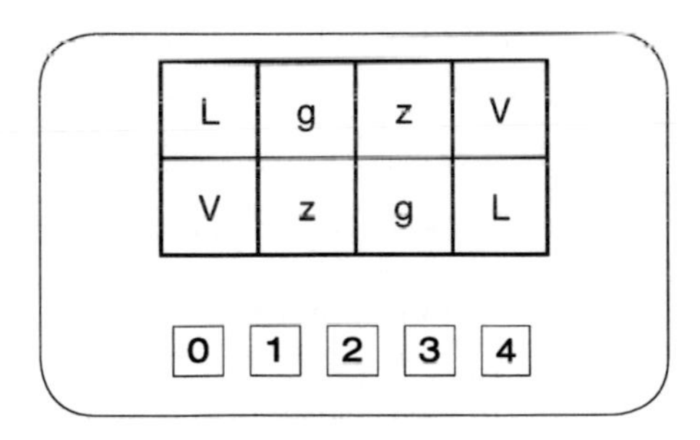

Now that you have completed the first Letter Checking exercise take the time to assess your performance with the answers below. If you got any wrong make sure you return to the question and see where you need to improve.

Once you are satisfied move onto exercise number 2.

ANSWERS TO LETTER CHECKING TEST - EXERCISE 1

1. 3

2. 3

3. 3

4. 4

5. 2

6. 3

7. 4

8. 1

9. 3

10. 3

11. 4

12. 3

13. 0

14. 3

15. 0

LETTER CHECKING TEST - EXERCISE 2

Question 1

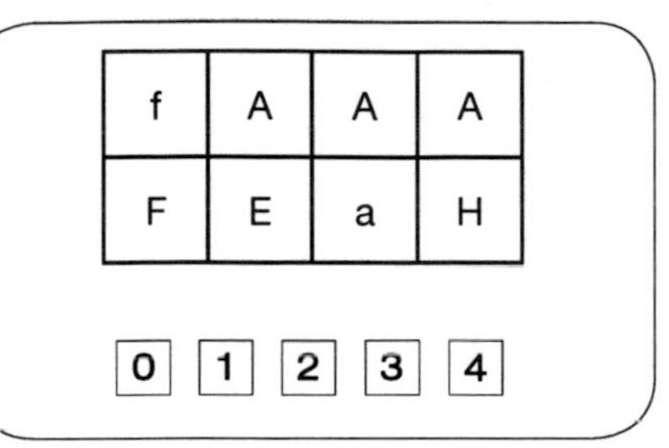

Question 2

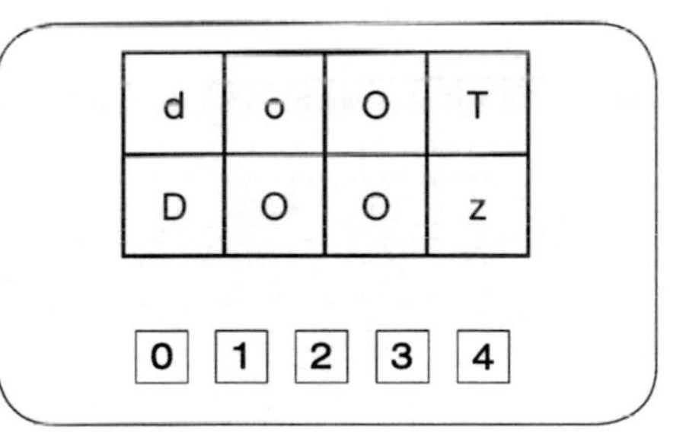

Question 3

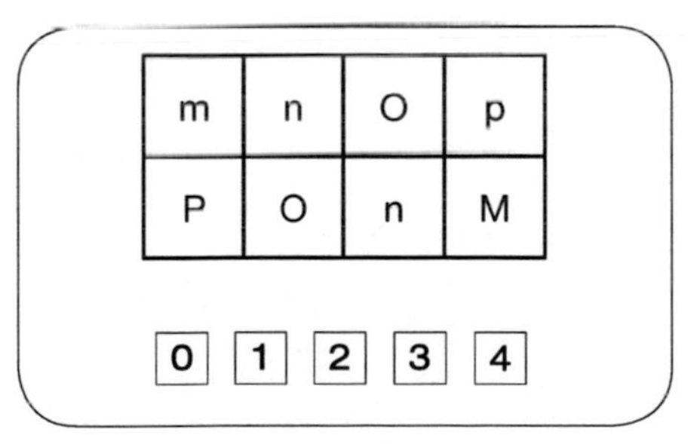

Question 4

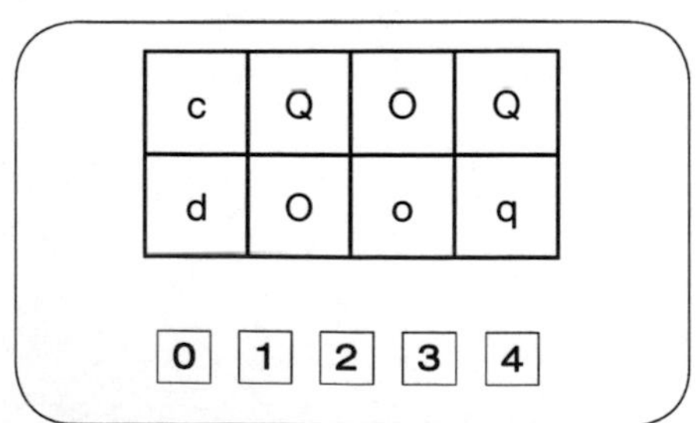

Question 5

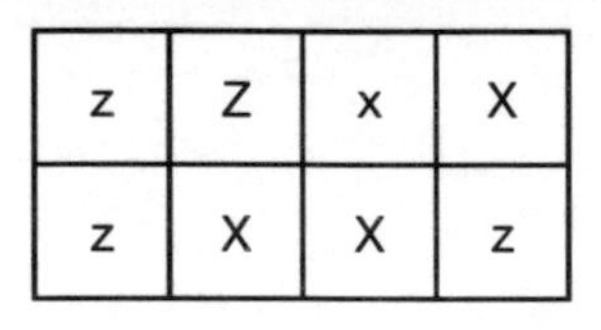

0 1 2 3 4

Question 6

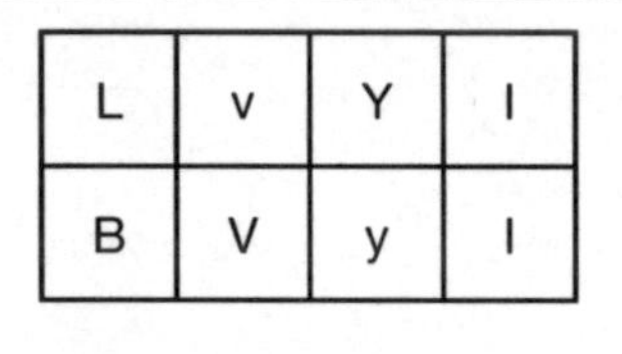

0 1 2 3 4

Question 7

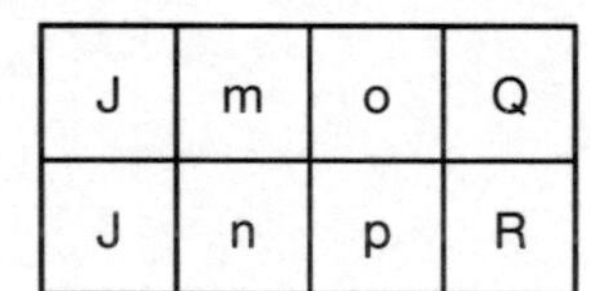

0 1 2 3 4

Question 8

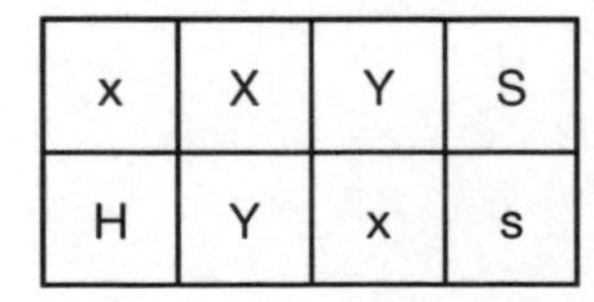

0 1 2 3 4

Question 9

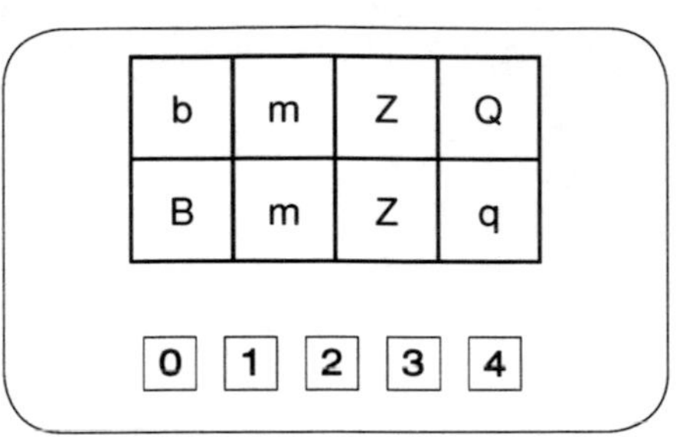

Question 10

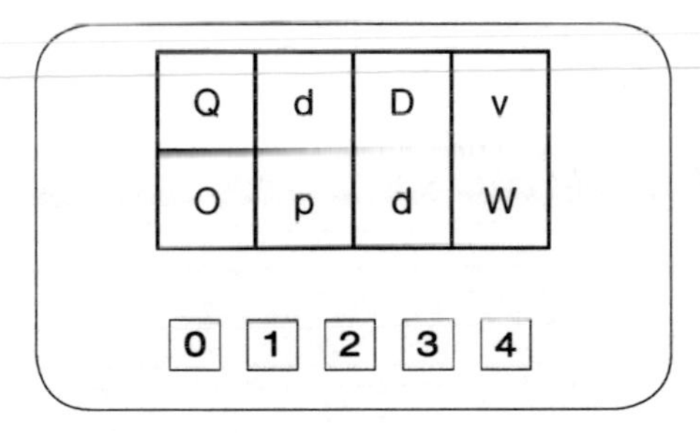

Question 11

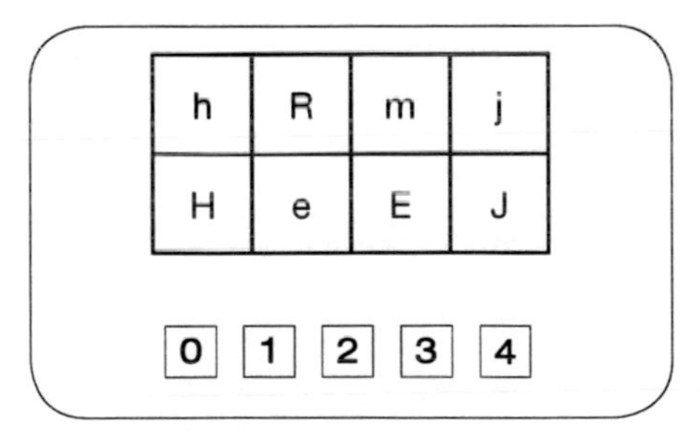

Question 12

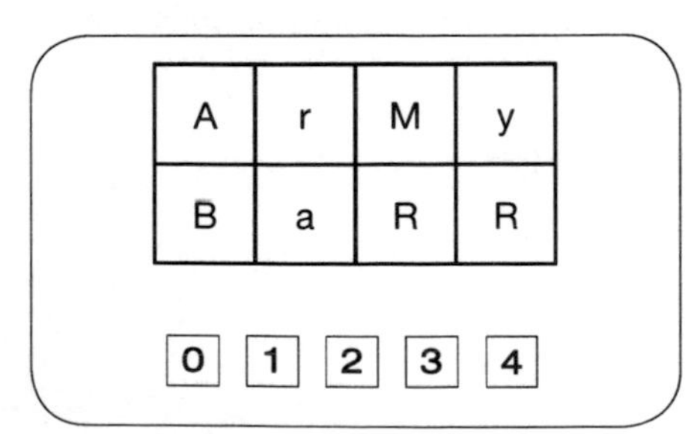

Question 13

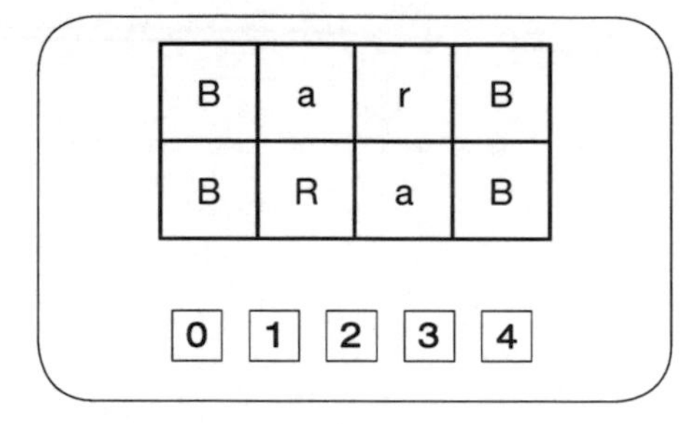

Question 14

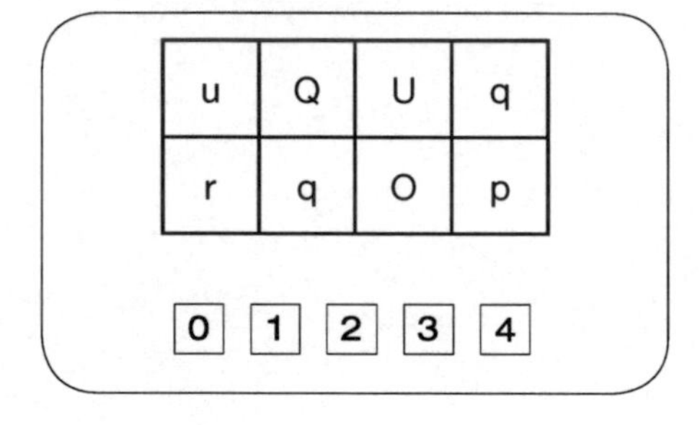

Question 15

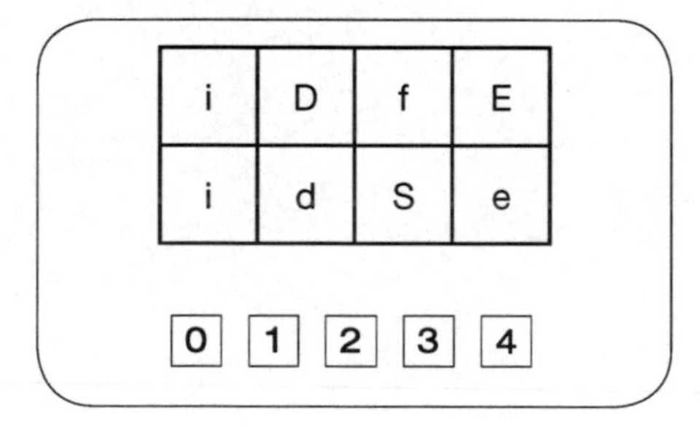

Once again, take the time to assess your performance with the answers below. If you got any wrong make sure you return to the question and see where you need to improve.

Once you are satisfied move onto the next exercise.

ANSWERS TO LETTER CHECKING TEST - EXERCISE 2

1. 2

2. 3

3. 0

4. 2

5. 2

6. 3

7. 1

8. 1

9. 4

10. 1

11. 2

12. 0

13. 2

14. 1

15. 3

LETTER CHECKING TEST - EXERCISE 3

Question 1

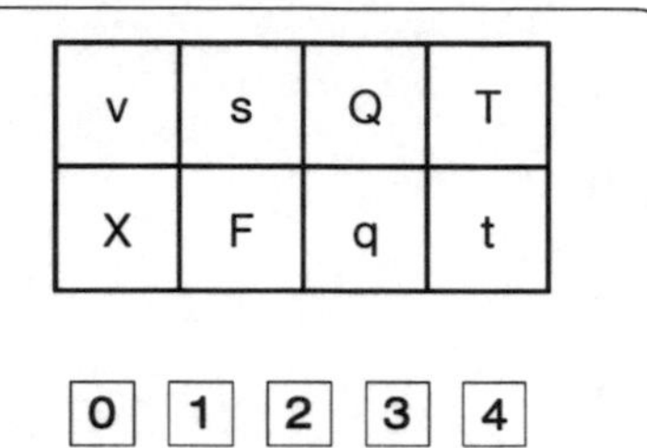

v	s	Q	T
X	F	q	t

0 1 2 3 4

Question 2

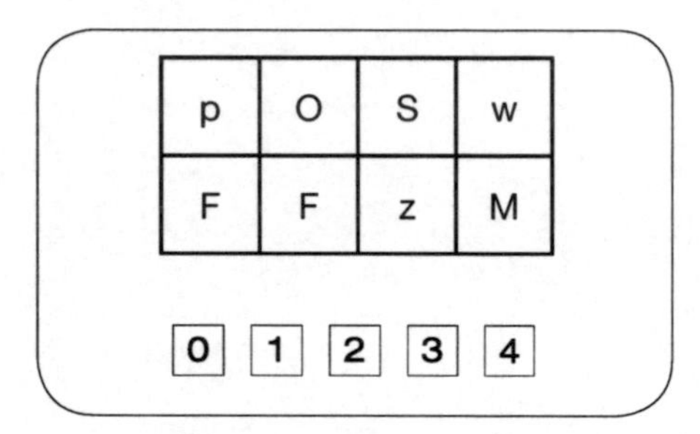

p	O	S	w
F	F	z	M

0 1 2 3 4

Question 3

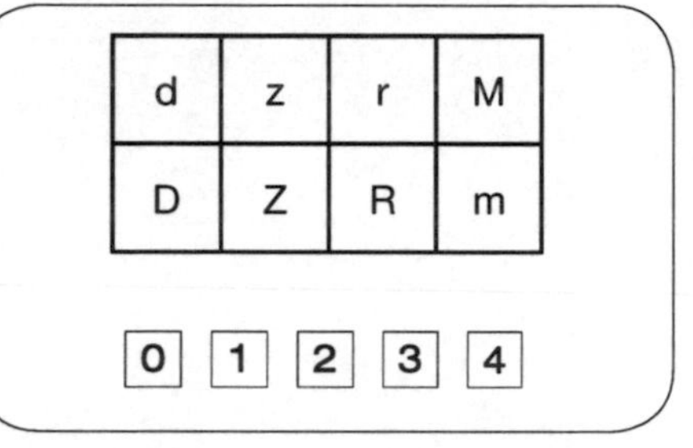

d	z	r	M
D	Z	R	m

0 1 2 3 4

Question 4

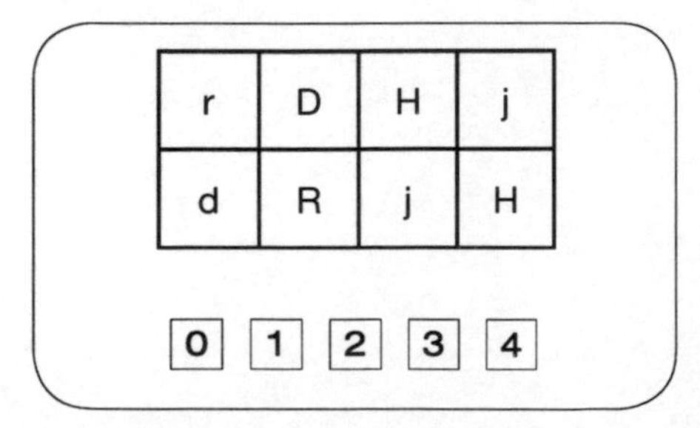

r	D	H	j
d	R	j	H

0 1 2 3 4

Question 5

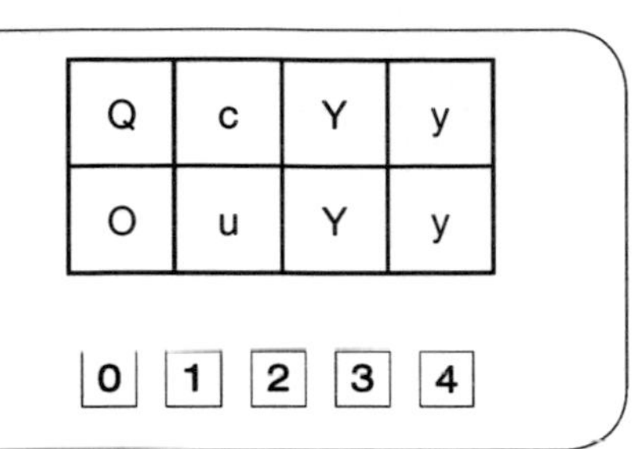

Question 6

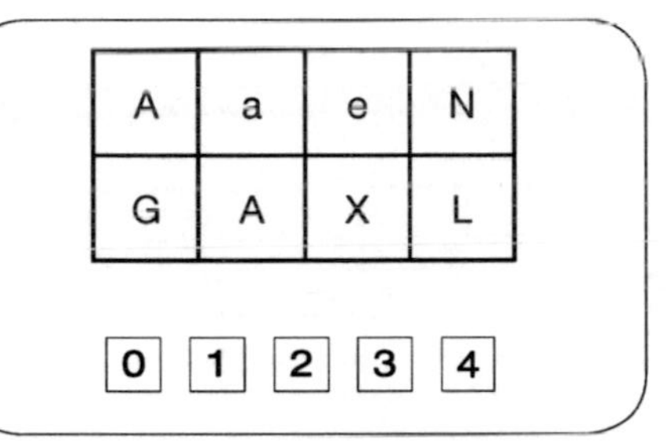

Question 7

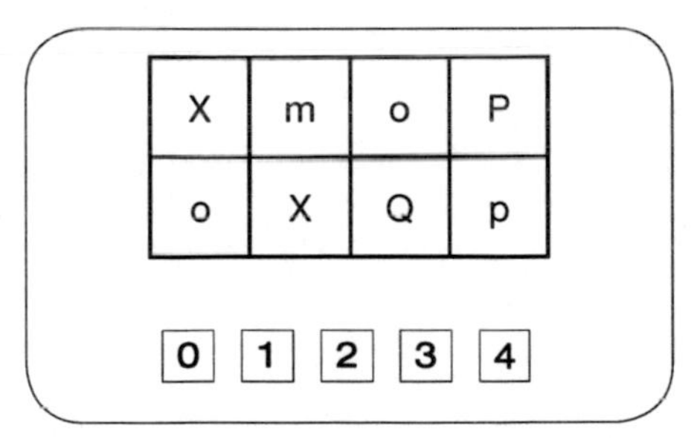

Question 8

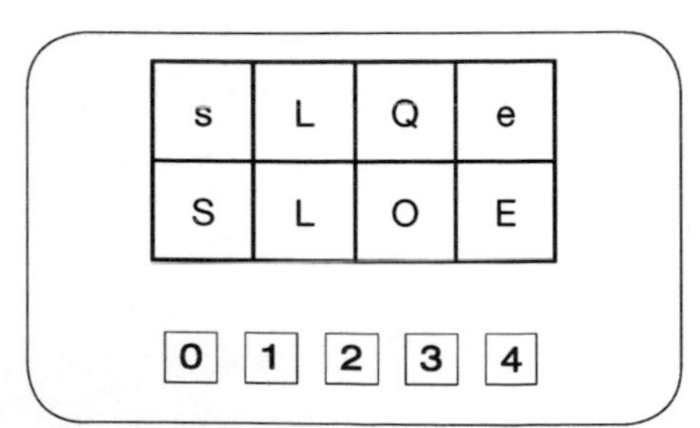

Question 9

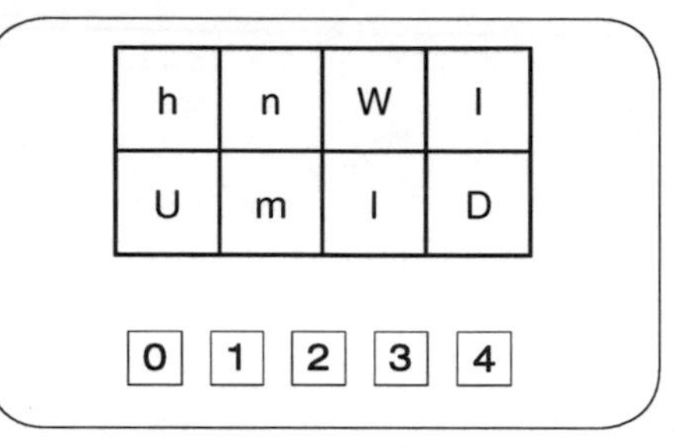

Question 10

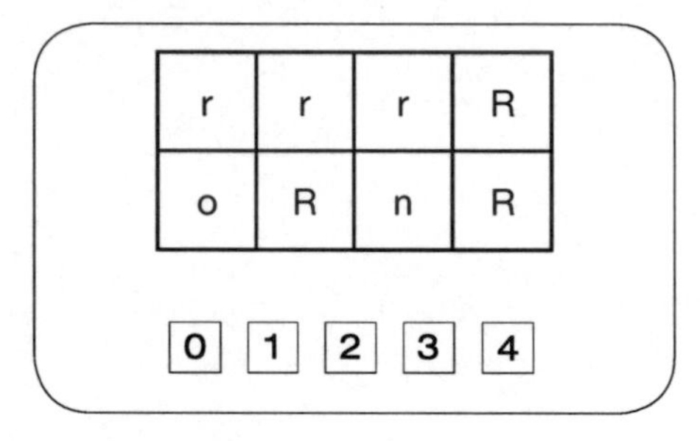

Question 11

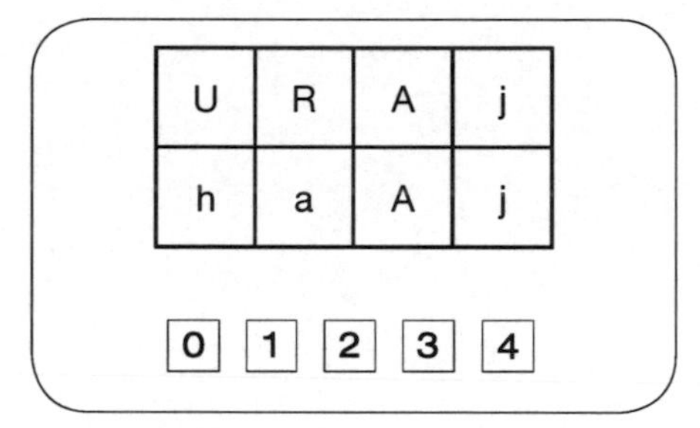

Question 12

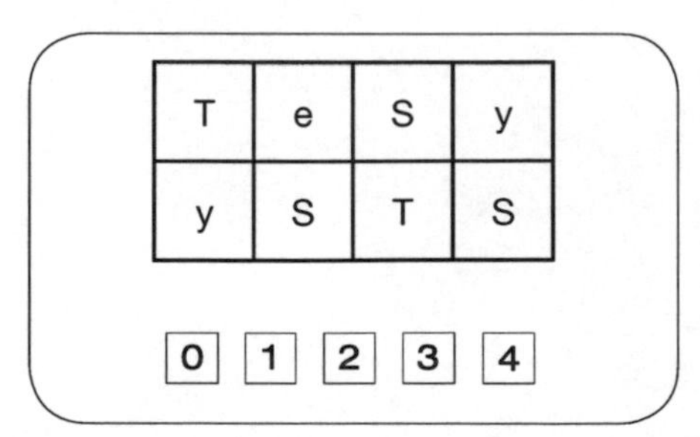

Question 13

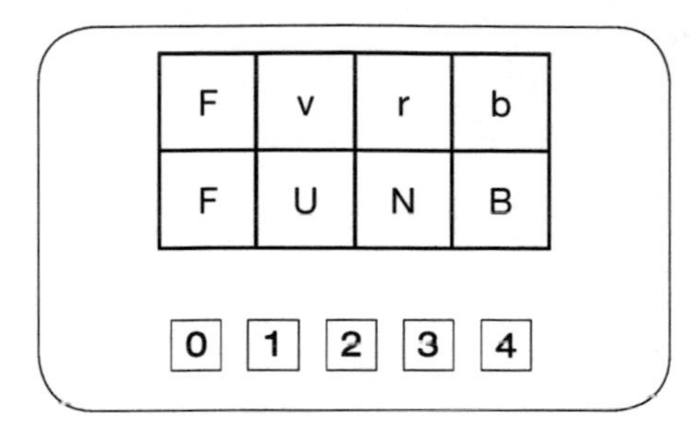

Question 14

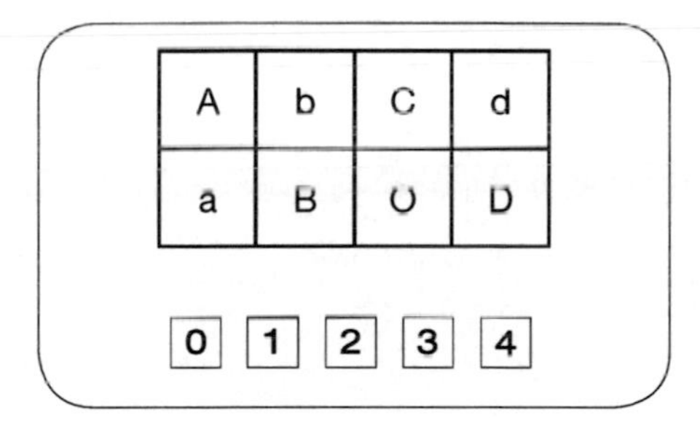

Question 15

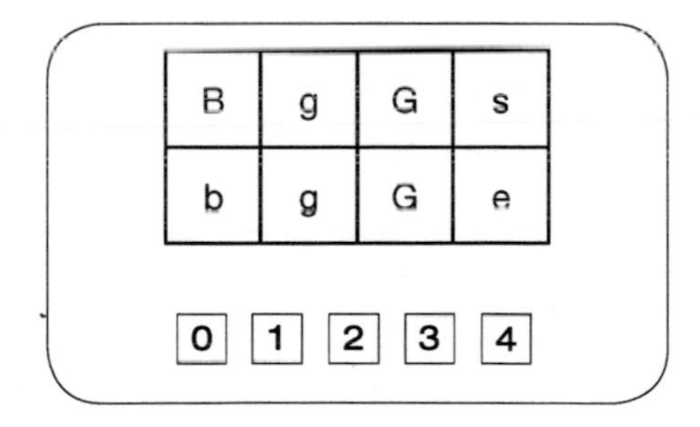

Once again, take the time to assess your performance with the answers below. If you got any wrong make sure you return to the question and see where you need to improve.

Once you are satisfied move onto the next section of the BARB test.

ANSWERS TO LETTER CHECKING TEST - EXERCISE 3

1. 2

2. 0

3. 4

4. 0

5. 2

6. 1

7. 1

8. 3

9. 0

10. 2

11. 2

12. 0

13. 2

14. 3

15. 3

CHAPTER 3
THE DISTANCE NUMBER TEST

During the BARB Test you will have to sit what is called a Distance Number test. This test requires you to analyse three numbers and decide which one of the three fits a certain criteria. For example, you may find 3 numbers appear on your computer screen as follows:

7 10 14

The numbers can appear in any order and will not necessarily increase in value as indicated above. You then have to analyse the numbers and decide which one is the largest number and which one is the smallest.

In this case that would be as follows:

Largest Value = 14

Smallest value = 7

This then leaves you with the number 10. Once you have decided which number remains (in this case the number 10) you then must decide which

of the two numbers (7 and 14) is the furthest away from it, hence the title 'Distance Number' test. To work this out you can see that 7 is 3 away from 10 but 14 is 4 away from 10, therefore leaving you with the answer 14.

This may seem complicated at first but with a little practice you will soon grasp the concept of what is required. As with all types of assessment test, the best way to improve your score is to prepare and practise. Try as many practice questions as possible and you will find that your scores will keep increasing.

On the following pages I have provided you with a number of sample questions for you to prepare. Before you start the test take a look at the following four step approach that will help you to answer the questions.

STEP 1

Out of the three numbers, decide which one is the smallest and which one is the largest.

STEP 2

Then look at the number you are left with.

STEP 3

Now decide which of the two numbers in step 1 is furthest away from the number in step 2

STEP 4

The number that is the furthest away is your answer.

Now move on to exercise 1. There are 30 questions for you to try and you have 15 minutes in which to answer them. The times that are provided in this test are different to times allocated in the real test.

DISTANCE NUMBER TEST - EXERCISE 1

Question 1

3 7 9

Answer

Question 2

4 8 2

Answer

Question 3

1 3 4

Answer

Question 4

10 15 19

Answer

Question 5

6 2 9

Answer

Question 6

7 13 12

Answer

Question 7

67 87 106

Answer

Question 8

2 1 4

Answer

Question 9

12 6 1

Answer

Question 10

4 9 6

Answer

Question 11

5 10 16

Answer

Question 12

100 101 98

Answer

Question 13

2 4 8

Answer

Question 14

14 21 8

Answer

Question 15

99 108 120

Answer

Question 16

7 2 13

Answer

Question 17

14 17 12

Answer

Question 18

9 7 13

Answer

Question 19

11 22 31

Answer

Question 20

98 90 80

Answer

Question 21

5 3 8

Answer

Question 22

15 4 10

Answer

Question 23

65 60 72

Answer

Question 24

45 38 30

Answer

Question 25

12 8 3

Answer

Question 26

108 208 18

Answer

Question 27

7 13 5

Answer

Question 28

3 8 5

Answer

Question 29

19 6 13

Answer

Question 30

2 9 17

Answer

Now that you have completed the first Distance Number exercise work through your answers checking carefully to see which, if any, you got wrong.

ANSWERS TO DISTANCE NUMBER TEST - EXERCISE 1

1. 3
2. 8
3. 1
4. 10
5. 2
6. 7
7. 67
8. 4
9. 12
10. 9
11. 16
12. 98
13. 8
14. 21
15. 120
16. 13
17. 17
18. 13
19. 11
20. 80
21. 8
22. 4
23. 72
24. 30
25. 3
26. 208
27. 13
28. 8
29. 6
30. 17

Now move on to exercise 2. Again, there are 30 questions for you to try and you have 15 minutes in which to answer them. The times that are provided in this test are different to times allocated in the real test.

DISTANCE NUMBER TEST - EXERCISE 2

Question 1

15 4 8

Answer

Question 2

2 6 9

Answer

Question 3

11 7 14

Answer

Question 4

1 19 3

Answer

Question 5

16 11 17

Answer

Question 6

8 3 9

Answer

Question 7

99 89 77

Answer

Question 8

267 16 134

Answer

Question 9

97 50 25

Answer

Question 10

45 44 42

Answer

Question 11

15	3	29

Answer

Question 12

66	14	33

Answer

Question 13

104	135	167

Answer

Question 14

474	300	122

Answer

Question 15

9	8	34

Answer

Question 16

90 45 3

Answer

Question 17

808 10 807

Answer

Question 18

1 55 101

Answer

Question 19

2 22 44

Answer

Question 20

65 99 128

Answer

Question 21

0 53 105

Answer

Question 22

36 2 17

Answer

Question 23

1001 501 2

Answer

Question 24

7 63 6

Answer

Question 25

809 799 698

Answer

Question 26

48 25 1

Answer

Question 27

5 16 25

Answer

Question 28

788 3 1574

Answer

Question 29

1000 100 599

Answer

Question 30

1971 11 1961

Answer

Now that you have completed Distance Number exercise 2 work through your answers once again checking carefully to see which, if any, you got wrong.

ANSWERS TO DISTANCE NUMBER TEST - EXERCISE 2

1. 15
2. 2
3. 14
4. 19
5. 11
6. 3
7. 77
8. 267
9. 97
10. 42
11. 29
12. 66
13. 167
14. 122
15. 34
16. 90
17. 10
18. 1
19. 44
20. 65
21. 0
22. 36
23. 1001
24. 63
25. 698
26. 1
27. 5
28. 1574
29. 100
30. 11

The Distance Number test, as previously stated, is designed to test your ability to quickly and accurately perform tasks in your head. A good way to practise is to carry out basic addition and subtraction exercises without the use or aid of a calculator. You will find that by just carrying out 10 minute exercises each day you will improve your response times greatly.

On the following pages I have provided you with some numerical reasoning tests to assist you in your preparation. Please note that these tests are not the type that you will come across in the BARB test and they should be used as a practice facility only. There are 30 questions for you to work through and you have 15 minutes in which to complete them. Calculators are not permitted. Simply circle your choice of answer using a pen or pencil.

PRACTICE NUMERACY TEST

Question 1

37 + ? = 95

A. 85 B. 45 C. 58 D. 57 E. 122

Question 2

86 - ? = 32

A. 54 B. 45 C. 108 D. 118 E. 68

Question 3

? + 104 = 210

A. 601 B. 314 C. 61 D.106 E.110

Question 4

109 x ? = 218

A. 1 B. 109 C. 12 D. 10 E. 2

Question 5

6 + 9 + 15 = 15 x ?

A. 15 B. 2 C. 3 D. 4 E. 5

Question 6

(34 + 13) – 4 = ? + 3

A. 7 B. 47 C. 51 D. 40 E. 37

Question 7

35 ÷ ? = 10 + 7.5

A. 2 B. 10 C. 4 D. 1 E. 17

Question 8

7 x ? = 28 x 3

A. 2 B. 3 C. 21 D. 15 E. 12

Question 9

100 ÷ 4 = 67 - ?

A. 42 B. 24 C. 57 D. 333 E. 2

Question 10

32 x 9 = 864 ÷ ?

A. 288 B. 3 C. 882 D. 4 E. None of these

Question 11

Following the pattern shown in the number sequence below, what is the missing number?

1 3 9 ? 81 243

A. 18 B. 27 C. 49 D. 21 E. 63

Question 12

If you count from 1 to 100, how many 6s will you pass on the way?

A.10 B. 19 C. 20 D. 11 E. 21

Question 13

50% of 350 equals?

A170 B. 25 C. 175 D. 170 E. 700

Question 14

75% of 1000 equals?

A. 75 B. 0.75 C. 75000 D. 750 E. 7.5

Question 15

40% of 40 equals?

A. 160 B. 4 C. 1600 D. 1.6 E. 16

Question 16

25% of 75 equals?

A. 18 B. 18.75 C. 18.25 D. 25 E. 17.25

Question 17

15% of 500 equals?

A. 75 B. 50 C. 0.75 D. 0.505 E. 750

Question 18

5% of 85 equals?

A. 4 B. 80 C. 4.25 D. 0.85 E. 89.25

Question 19

9876 – 6789 equals?

A. 3078 B. 3085 C. 783 D. 3086 E. 3087

Question 20

27 x 4 equals?

A. 106 B. 107 C. 108 D. 109 E. 110

Question 21

96 ÷ 4 equals?

A. 22 B. 23 C. 24 D. 25 E. 26

Question 22

8765 – 876 equals?

A. 9887 B. 7888 C. 7890 D. 7998 E. 7889

Question 23

623 + 222 equals?

A. 840 B. 845 C. 740 D. 745 E. 940

Question 24

A rectangle has an area of 24cm^2 . The length of one side is 8cm. What is the perimeter of the rectangle?

A. 22 inches B. 24cm C. 18cm D. 22cm E. 18 inches

Question 25

A square has a perimeter of 36cm. Its area is 81cm². What is the length of one side?

A. 9cm B. 18cm C. 9 metres D. 18 metres E. 16cm

Question 26

Which of the following is the same as 25/1000?

A. 0.25 B. 0.025 C. 0.0025 D. 40 E. 25000

Question 27

Is 33 divisible by 3?

A. Yes B. No

Question 28

What is 49% of 1100?

A. 535 B. 536 C. 537 D. 538 E. 539

Question 29

One side of a rectangle is 12cm. If the area of the rectangle is 84cm2, what is the length of the shorter side?

A. 5cm B. 6cm C. 7cm D. 8cm E. 9cm

Question 30

A rectangle has an area of 8cm2. The length of one side is 2cm. What is the perimeter?

A. 4cm B. 6cm C. 8cm D. 10cm E. None of these.

Now that you have completed the sample numeracy test work through your answers carefully before moving onto the next section of the BARB test.

ANSWERS TO PRACTICE NUMERACY TEST

1. C
2. A
3. D
4. E
5. B
6. D
7. A
8. E
9. A
10. A
11. B
12. C
13. C
14. D
15. E
16. C
17. A
18. C
19. E
20. C
21. C
22. E
23. B
24. D
25. A
26. B
27. A
28. E
29. C
30. E

CHAPTER 4
THE SELECTING THE ODD ONE OUT TEST

As part of the BARB test you will be required to sit a selecting the Odd One Out test. The requirement of this test is to simply select the odd one out from a group of words. Take a look at the following sample question:

Sample question

Which of the following is the odd one out?

Ball **Footballer** **Tree**

The answer to this question is Tree. The reason is that Ball and Footballer are associated together, whereas Tree cannot be placed in the same category as the other two words, so therefore is the odd one out. You may find some words are the opposite of another one, which again is the association or connection. Here's another example.

Sample question

Which of the following is the odd one out?

Warm **Cold** **Car**

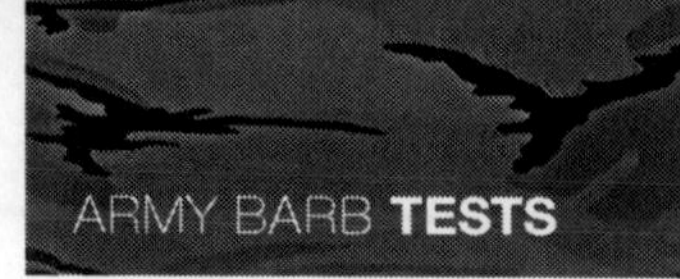

The odd one out in this example is Car. Warm is opposite to Cold, so therefore Car is the odd one out. Now try the exercise on the following page.

Remember to read the questions carefully. When you sit the real test with the Army you may have to take the test on a computer as described in previous pages. An example of a question presented on a computer screen would be as follows:

In this particular question **River** is the odd one out. Allow yourself 2 minutes only to answer as many questions as possible on the following exercise which contains 14 questions. Simply circle which word you believe is the odd one out. Once again the times provided in this sample test are different to the real test.

SELECTING THE ODD ONE OUT - EXERCISE 1

Question 1

Bark Sun Tree

Question 2

Peanut Mechanic Spanner

Question 3

Hello Goodbye Running

Question 4

Plane Ship Centipede

Question 5

Kilo Gram Sugar

Question 6

Garage Swing Playground

Question 7

Poor	Rich	Grass

Question 8

You	Lady	Me

Question 9

Good	Table	Bad

Question 10

Little	Date	Large

Question 11

Wet	Dry	Ear

Question 12

Old	Young	Light

Question 13

Day Night Road

Question 14

Forever New Fresh

ANSWERS TO SELECTING THE ODD ONE OUT - EXERCISE 1

1. Sun

2. Peanut

3. Running

4. Centipede

5. Sugar

6. Garage

7. Grass

8. Lady

9. Table

10. Date

11. Ear

12. Light

13. Road

14. Forever

Once you have checked all of your answers thoroughly move on to the sample exercise 2 on the following page. In this exercise there are 14 questions and you have 2 minutes in which to complete them.

SELECTING THE ODD ONE OUT - EXERCISE 2

Question 1

Wheel	Art	Painting

Question 2

Sunny	Grass	Raining

Question 3

Kitchen	Attic	Sea

Question 4

Pie	Soup	Gravel

Question 5

Bike	Farmer	Pigs

Question 6

Computer	Can	Drink

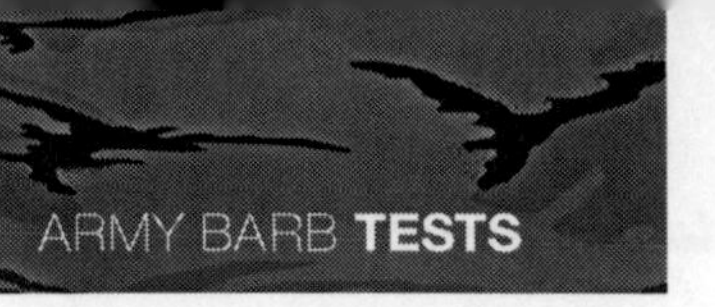

Question 7

Trousers	Running	Belt

Question 8

Men	Women	Army

Question 9

Horrible	Nice	Nasty

Question 10

Window	Glass	Cement

Question 11

Spoon	Red	Yellow

Question 12

Money	Car	Bank

Question 13

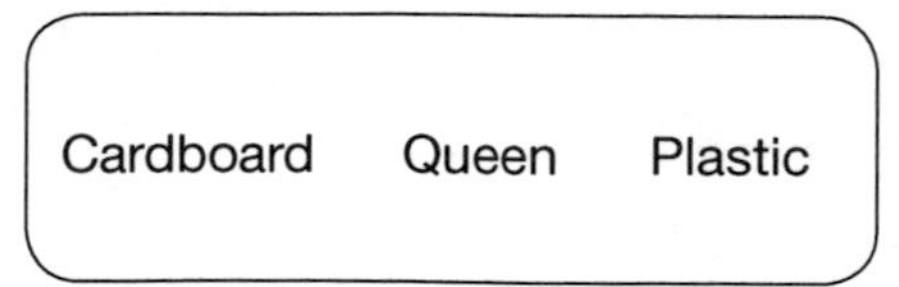

Question 14

Once you have completed exercise 2 work through your answers correcting any that you get wrong. Once you have done this simply move on to the next exercise.

ANSWERS TO SELECTING THE ODD ONE OUT - EXERCISE 2

1. Wheel

2. Grass

3. Sea

4. Gravel

5. Bike

6. Computer

7. Running

8. Army

9. Nice

10. Cement

11. Spoon

12. Car

13. Queen

14. Wooden

SELECTING THE ODD ONE OUT - EXERCISE 3

Question 1

Baby	Daylight	Cot

Question 2

Harsh	Firm	Soft

Question 3

Mortar	Sailing	Bricks

Question 4

Dream	Umpire	Cricket

Question 5

Repeat	Laces	Shoes

Question 6

Eat	Dine	Wrist

Question 7

Plate Brakes Car

Question 8

Telephone Communicate Motorway

Question 9

Reach Grab Desire

Question 10

Leaf Cow Pony

Question 11

Moisturiser Cream Distance

Question 12

Road Battle Truck

Question 13

Midnight Moon Castle

Question 14

Shed Baking Food

ANSWERS TO SELECTING THE ODD ONE OUT - EXERCISE 3

1. Daylight

2. Soft

3. Sailing

4. Dream

5. Repeat

6. Wrist

7. Plate

8. Motorway

9. Desire

10. Leaf

11. Distance

12. Battle

13. Castle

14. Shed

Once you have checked all of your answers thoroughly move on to the next section of the BARB test which is the symbol rotation test.

CHAPTER 5
THE SYMBOL ROTATION TEST

During the BARB test you will be required to sit the Symbol Rotation test. The requirement of this test is to identify which symbols are matching by rotation.

Take a look at the following 2 pairs of letters:

You will be able to see that both pairs of letters are the *same*. The only difference is that the letters have each been rotated. Now take a look at the next 2 pairs of letters:

You will see that if each letter on the top row is rotated through all angles, it is impossible to match it up with the bottom letter directly below it. Therefore the letters are said to be a *mirror* image of each other.

During the symbol rotation test you will be required to identify how many pairs of symbols are matching. You will have to rotate the letters/symbols in your mind and decide how many of the pairs that are presented in front of you actually match. Take a look at the following 3 pairs of letters and decide how many are matching:

SAMPLE QUESTION

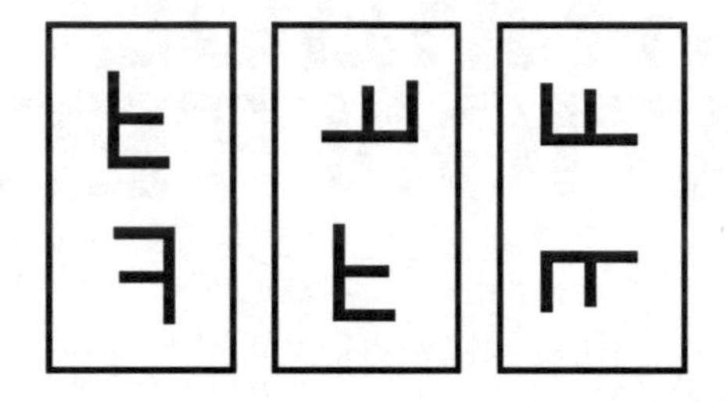

You will see that the letters in the first two boxes can be rotated round to match. The pair in the third box however cannot be rotated to match. Therefore there are two pairs in this sequence that are identical.

Now try the exercise on the following pages. Your task is to identify how many pairs of letters match in each sequence. You have 5 minutes to complete the exercise of 15 questions. Simply circle which answer is correct in the box beneath each question. The times provided in the following sample exercises are not the same as the real test.

SYMBOL ROTATION TEST – EXERCISE 1

Question 1

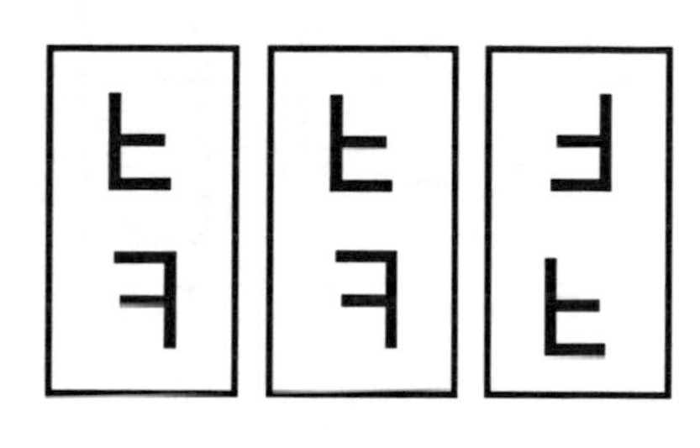

0 1 2 3

Question 2

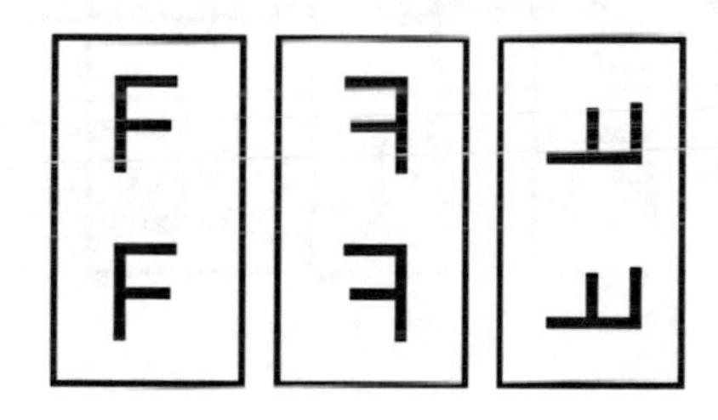

0 1 2 3

Question 3

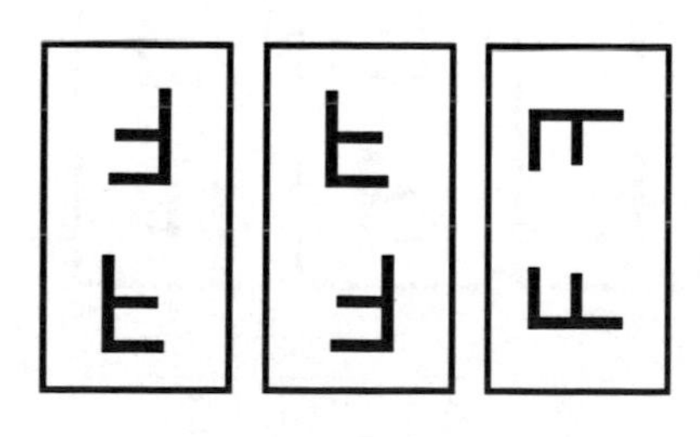

0 1 2 3

Question 4

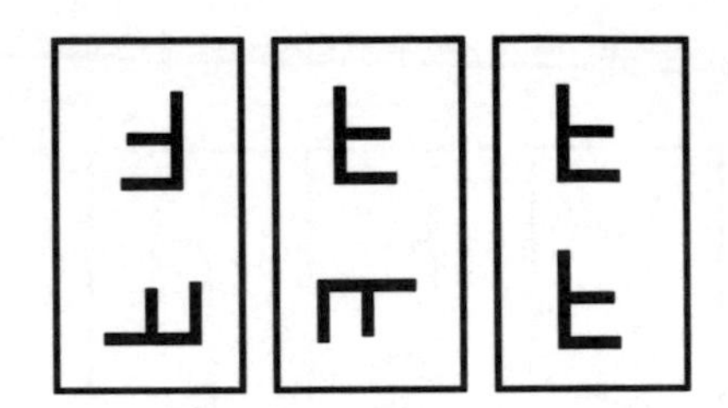

0 1 2 3

Question 5

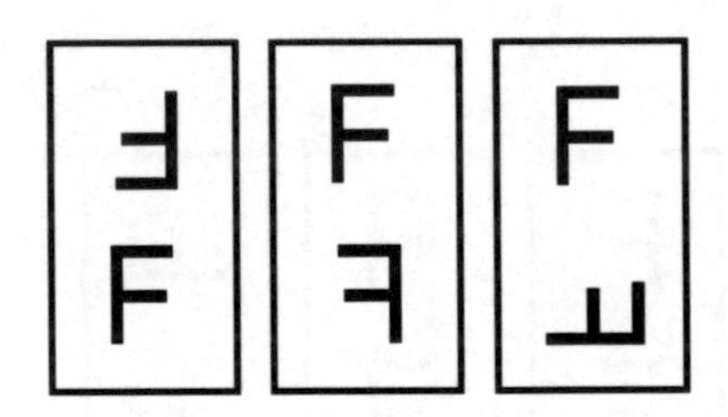

0 1 2 3

Question 6

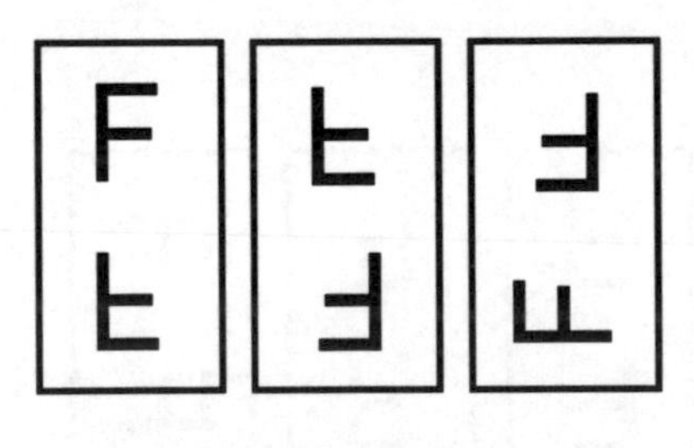

0 1 2 3

Question 7

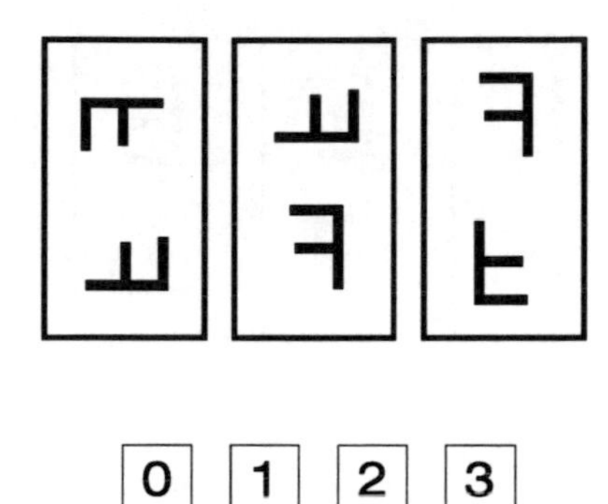

Question 8

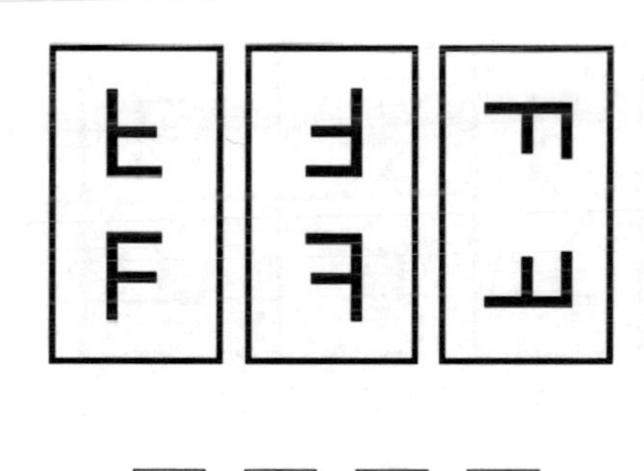

Question 9

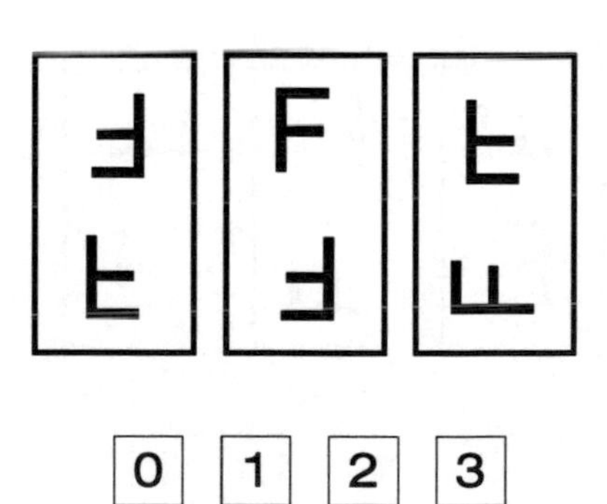

Question 10

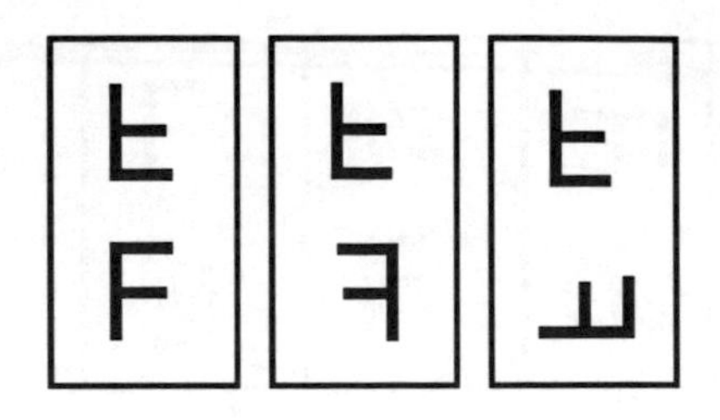

0 1 2 3

Question 11

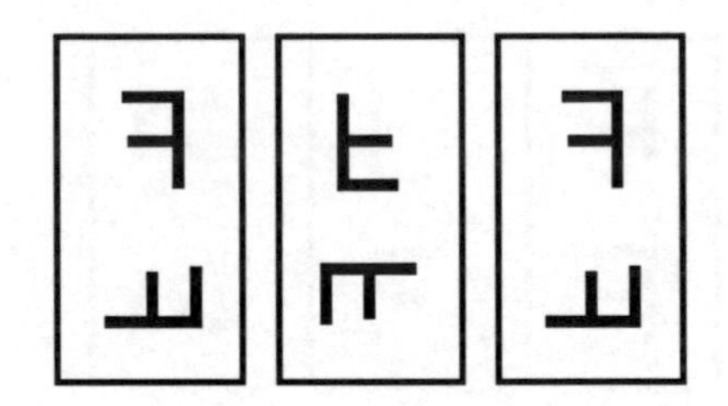

0 1 2 3

Question 12

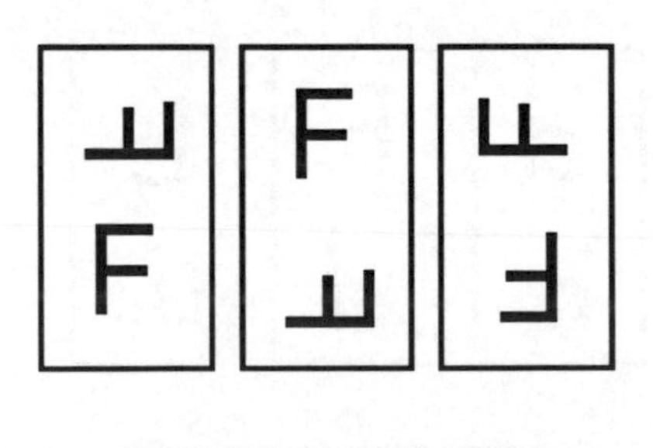

0 1 2 3

Question 13

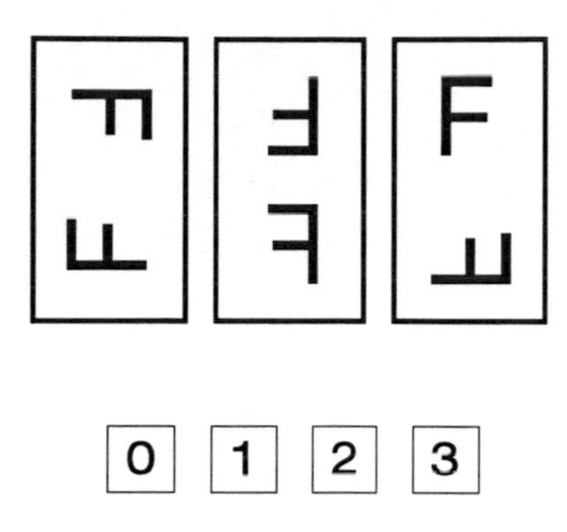

Question 14

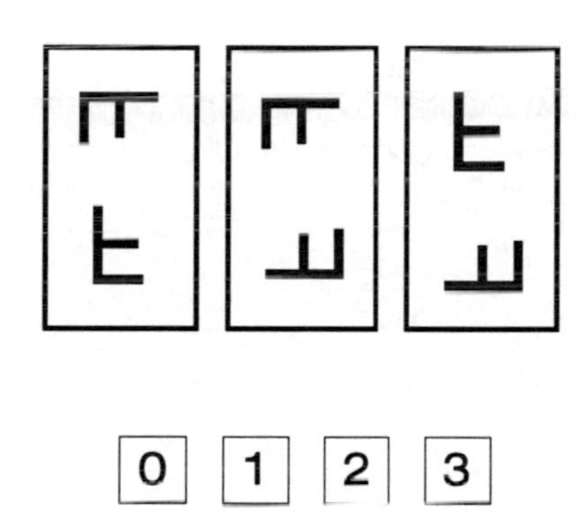

Question 15

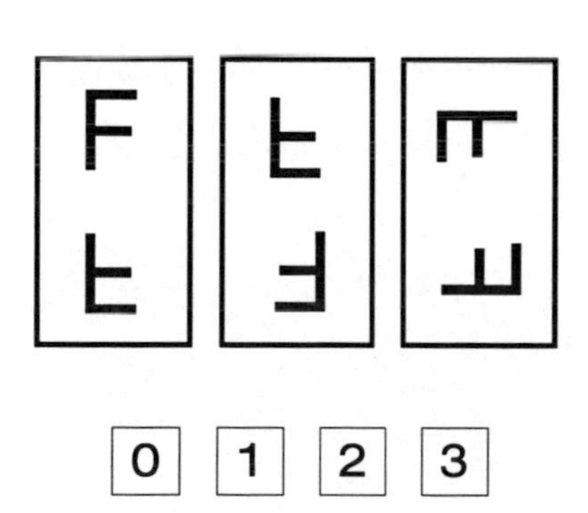

Now that you have completed the exercise take the time to check over your answers carefully before moving on to Symbol Rotation exercise 2.

ANSWERS TO SYMBOL ROTATION TEST - EXERCISE 1

1. 2

2. 3

3. 0

4. 2

5. 1

6. 1

7. 3

8. 0

9. 1

10. 2

11. 3

12. 1

13. 1

14. 3

15. 1

Now move on to the next exercise. Once again there are 15 questions and you have 5 minutes to work through them. Circle the correct answer in the box provided.

SYMBOL ROTATION TEST – EXERCISE 2

Question 1

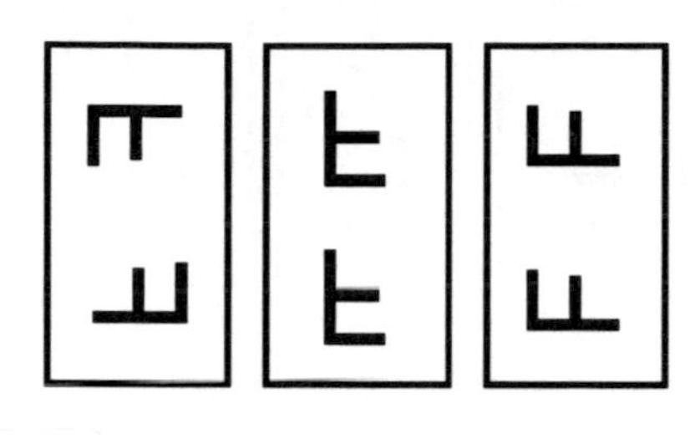

0 1 2 3

Question 2

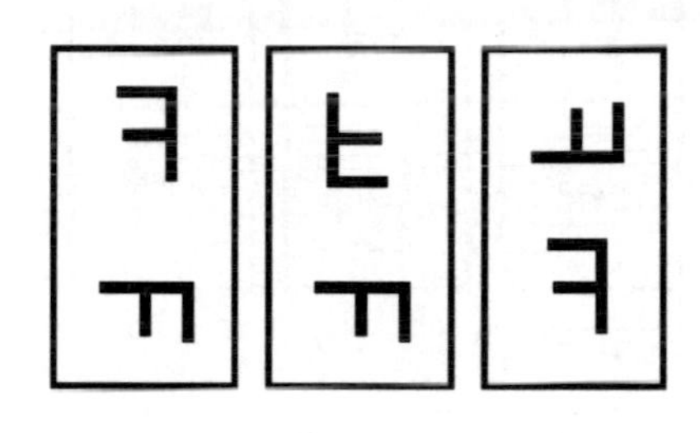

0 1 2 3

Question 3

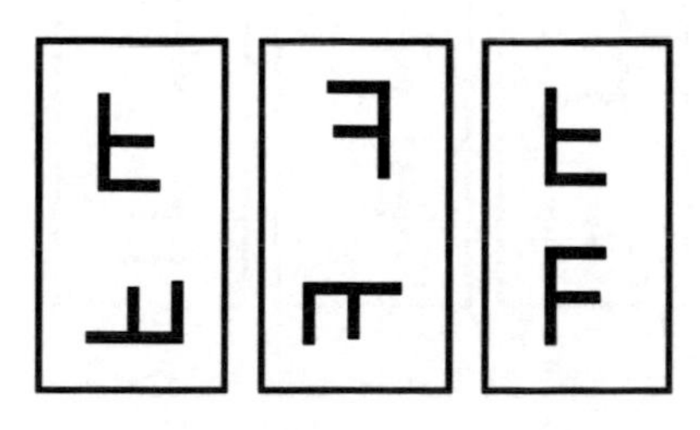

0 1 2 3

Question 4

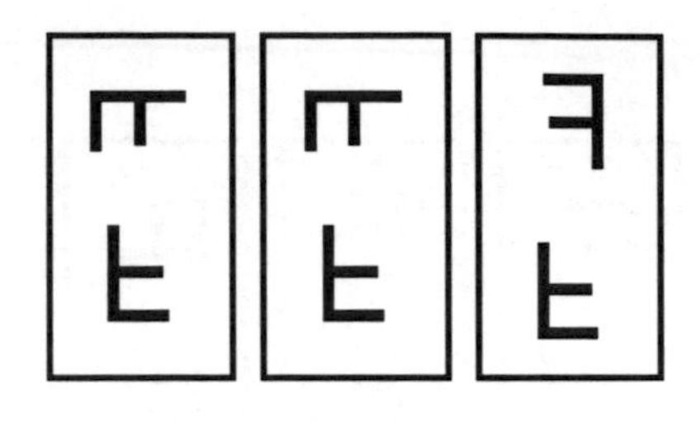

0 1 2 3

Question 5

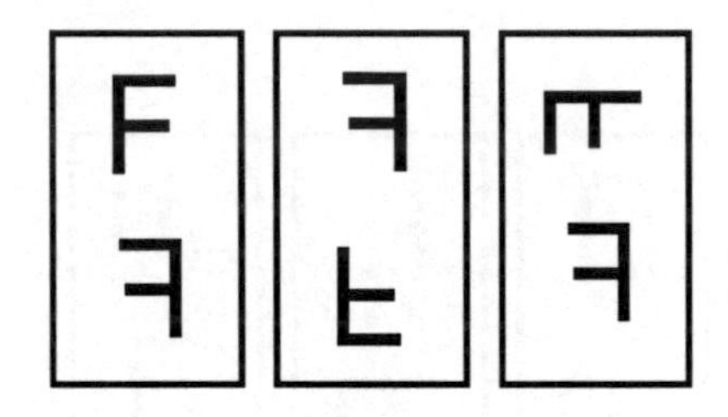

0 1 2 3

Question 6

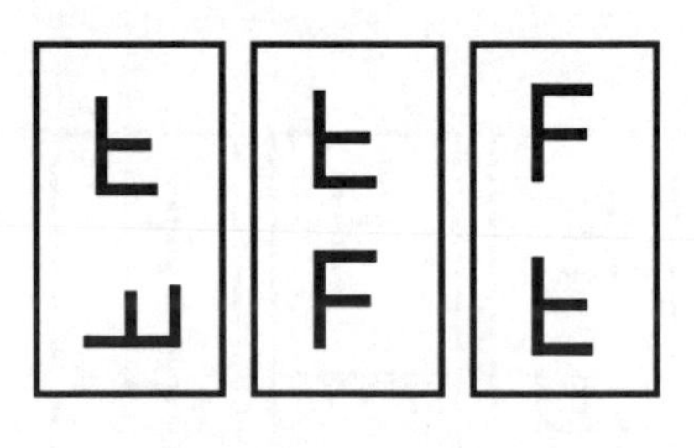

0 1 2 3

Question 7

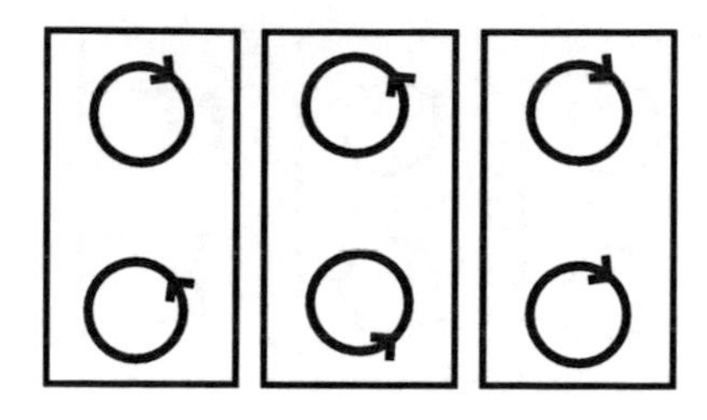

0 1 2 3

Question 8

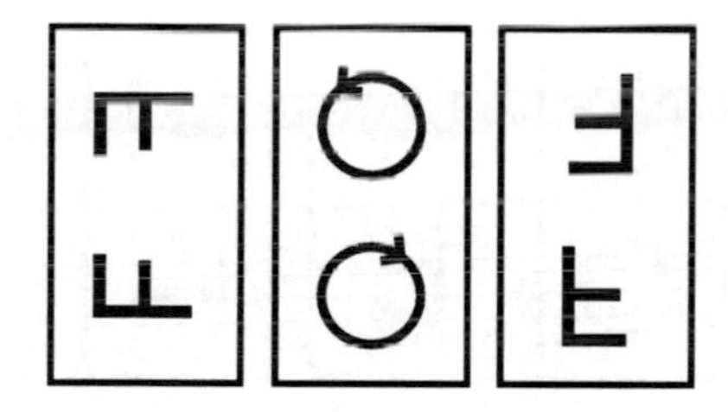

0 1 2 3

Question 9

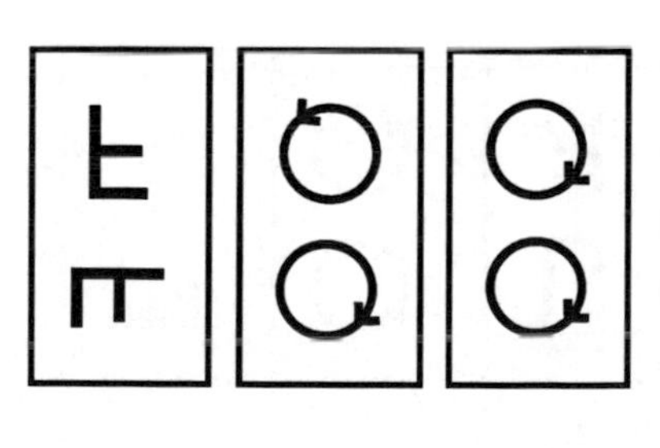

0 1 2 3

Question 10

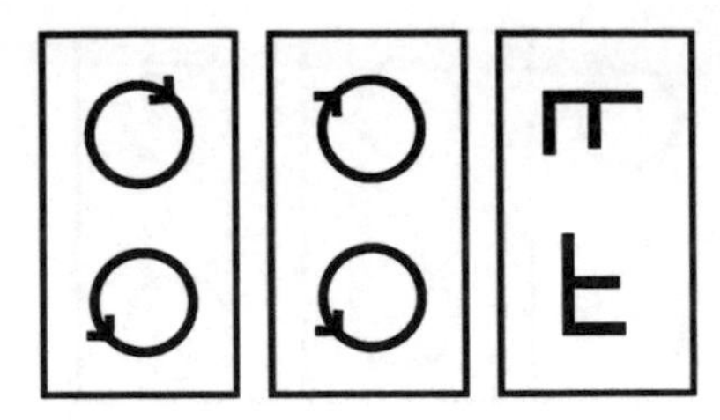

0 1 2 3

Question 11

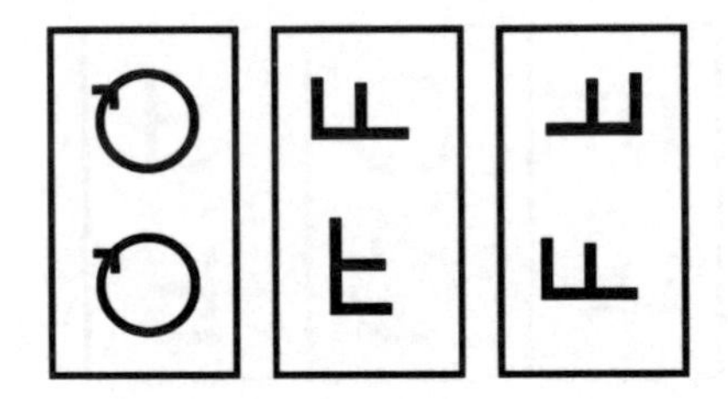

0 1 2 3

Question 12

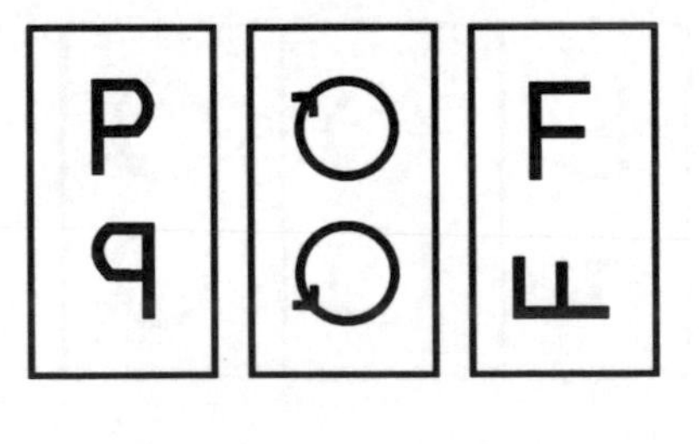

0 1 2 3

Question 13

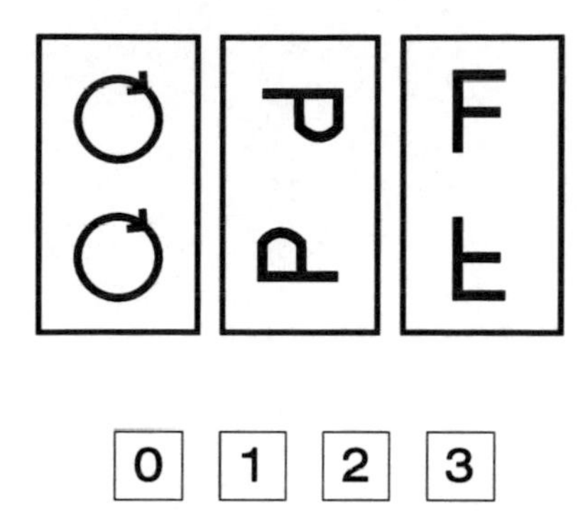

Question 14

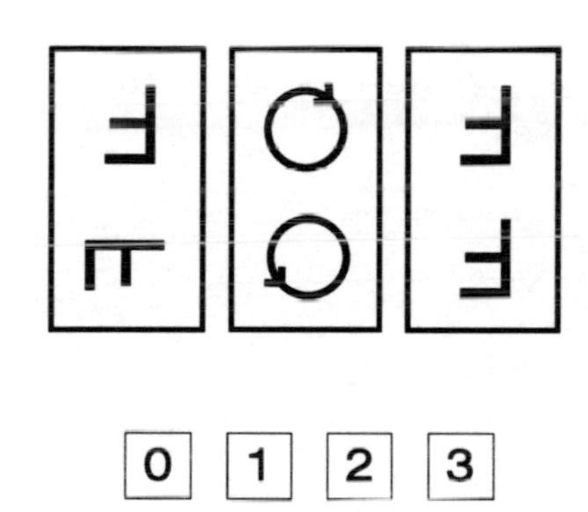

Question 15

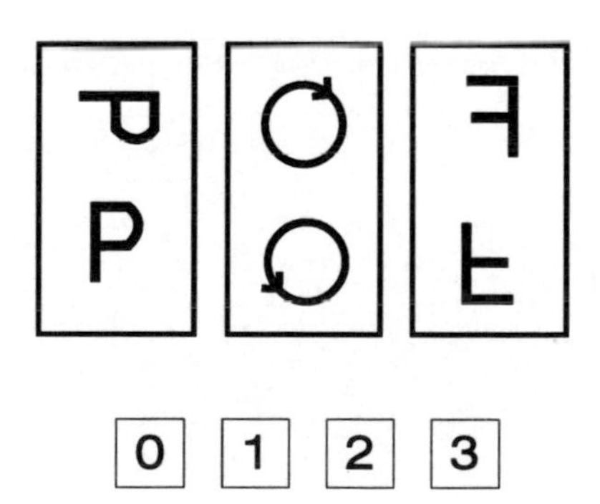

Now that you have completed the exercise take the time to check over your answers carefully before moving onto the next exercise.

ANSWERS TO SYMBOL ROTATION TEST - EXERCISE 2

1. 3
2. 1
3. 2
4. 3
5. 2
6. 1
7. 2
8. 0
9. 2
10. 1
11. 1
12. 1
13. 2
14. 1
15. 2

Now move on to the next exercise. There are 15 questions and you have 5 minutes to complete them.

SYMBOL ROTATION TEST – EXERCISE 3

Question 1

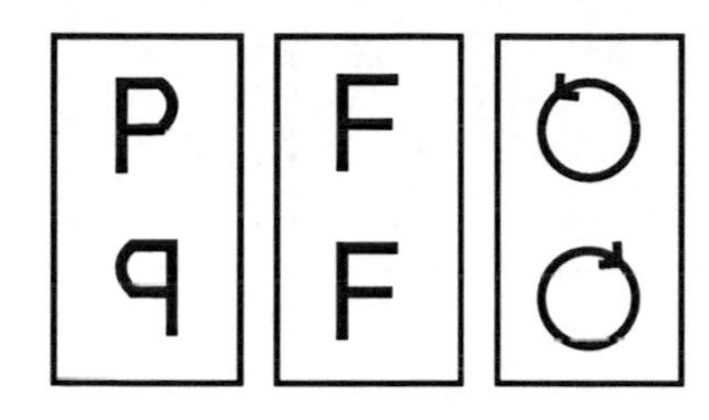

0 1 2 3

Question 2

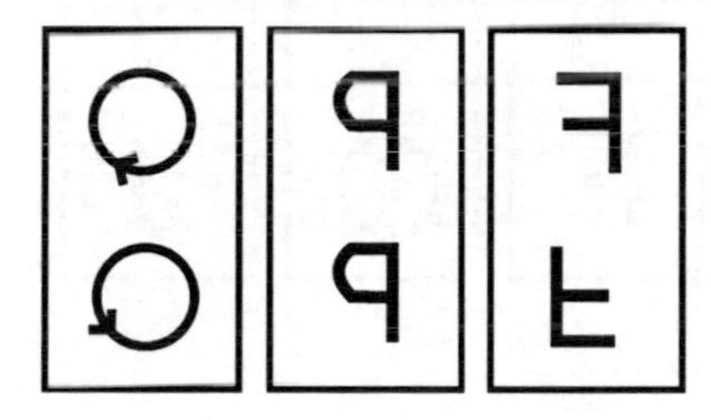

0 1 2 3

Question 3

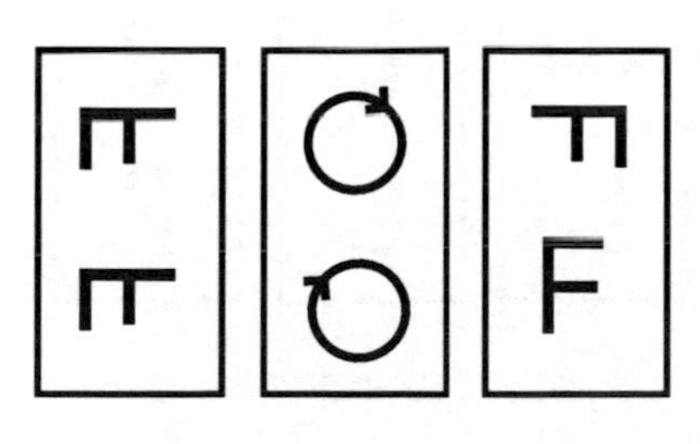

0 1 2 3

Question 4

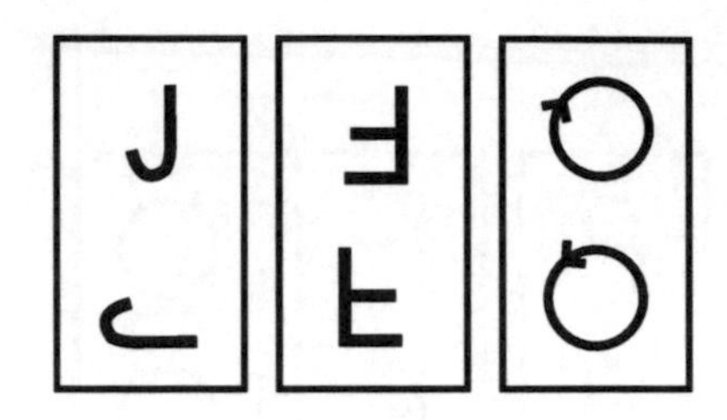

0 1 2 3

Question 5

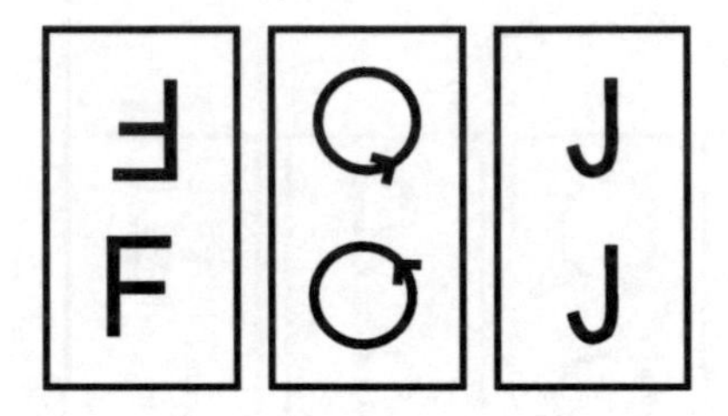

0 1 2 3

Question 6

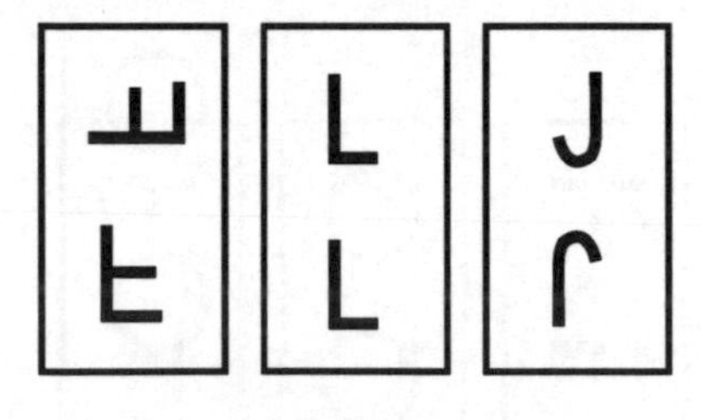

0 1 2 3

Question 7

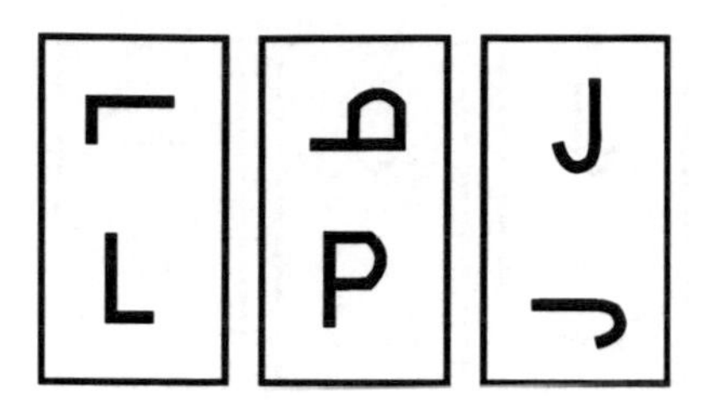

0 1 2 3

Question 8

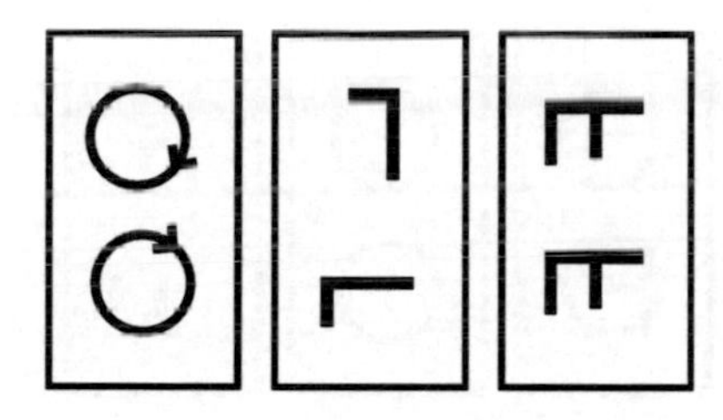

0 1 2 3

Question 9

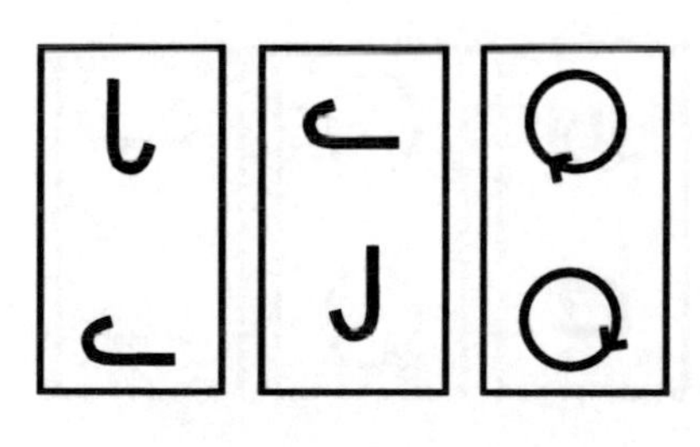

0 1 2 3

Question 10

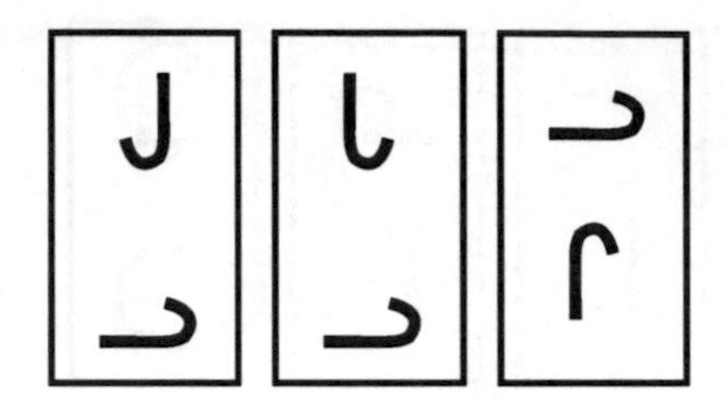

0 1 2 3

Question 11

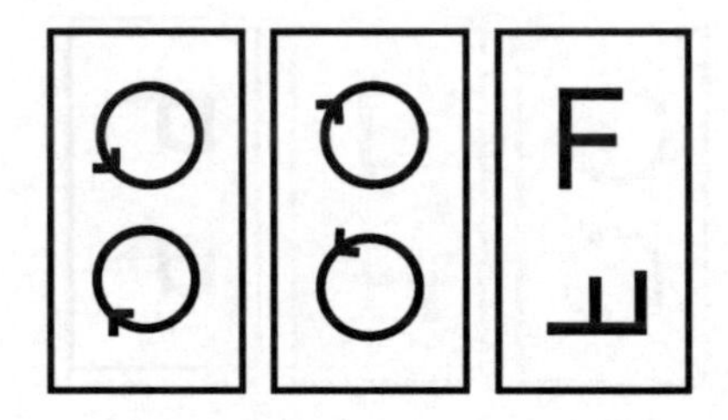

0 1 2 3

Question 12

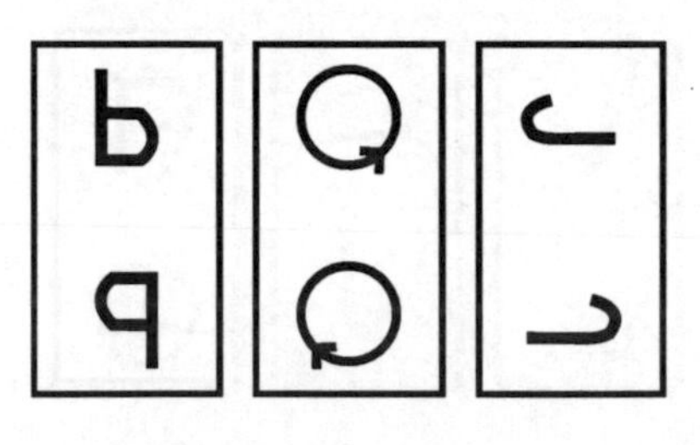

0 1 2 3

Question 13

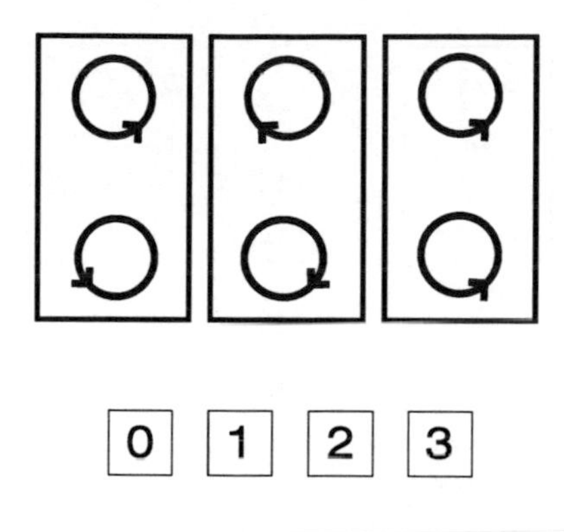

0 1 2 3

Question 14

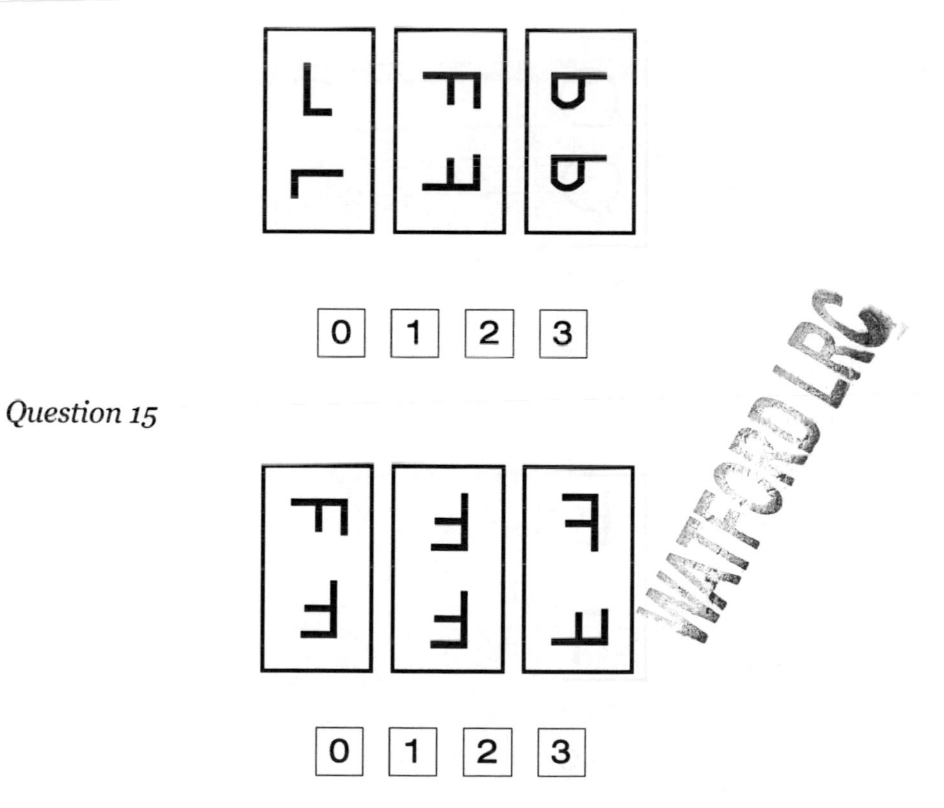

0 1 2 3

Question 15

0 1 2 3

Now that you have completed the exercise take the time to check over your answers carefully before moving on to the final tips for passing the BARB test.

ANSWERS TO SYMBOL ROTATION TEST - EXERCISE 3

1. 1

2. 2

3. 3

4. 1

5. 3

6. 3

7. 2

8. 3

9. 2

10. 1

11. 0

12. 1

13. 3

14. 2

15. 3

FINAL TIPS FOR PASSING THE BARB TEST

Success at the BARB test will be very much dependant on how much, and the type of preparation you carry out. Don't forget to make your preparation deliberate in the essence of carrying out plenty of repetitive practice in the areas that are your most weakest. For example, if you feel that you are poor at the Distance Number test then get yourself of copy of a numerical reasoning test booklet and work hard at the questions contained within it. If you really worried about your testing ability then I would recommend you consider obtaining a personal tutor to assist you. Your practice should be over a prolonged period of time but not by way of cramming the night before your test. Little and often is the key to success.

As previously stated you should take care of what you eat and drink in the build up to the test. Avoid alcohol and caffeine in the few days leading up to the test and get plenty of rest. You will want to be at your best during the test and all of these small areas will help you to improve your scores.

THE TESTING SERIES
expert advice on test preparation

how2become